THE FBI WAY

THE
FBI WAY

INSIDE THE BUREAU'S
CODE OF EXCELLENCE

FRANK FIGLIUZZI

CUSTOM
HOUSE

HarperCollins books may be purchased for educational, business, or sales promotional use. For information, please email the Special Markets Department at SPsales@harpercollins.com.

FIRST EDITION

Designed by Angela Boutin

Library of Congress Cataloging-in-Publication Data has been applied for.

ISBN 978-0-06-299705-0 (hardcover)
ISBN 978-0-06-306039-5 (international edition)

21 22 23 24 25 CPI 10 9 8 7 6 5 4 3 2 1

To the men and women
of the Federal Bureau of Investigation,
past, present, and future, who preserve our values
and defend our freedom

The only thing necessary for the triumph of
evil is for good men to do nothing.

—EDMUND BURKE

Excellence is never an accident.
It is always the result of high intention, sincere
effort, and intelligent execution; it represents
the wise choice of many alternatives—choice,
not chance, determines your destiny.

—ARISTOTLE

CONTENTS

THE FBI WAY

HOT WASH

I T WAS MY TURN TO BE THE FBI'S DESIGNATED SURVIVOR, an "honor" rotated among the Bureau's assistant directors. On a crisp night in January 2012, the future of the republic seemed to rest on my shoulders and those of the designees from other agencies, dozens of us packed into a heavily fortified bunker far outside Washington, D.C., at a location I still can't reveal.

Barack Obama was at the U.S. Capitol, delivering his State of the Union address, which meant that most of the president's cabinet, the justices of the Supreme Court, and members of the Senate and House of Representatives were in the chamber too. But not us. Joining me at that undisclosed location were a cabinet secretary, staffers from both the House and Senate, and a handful of buttoned-down middle-aged officials from key federal agencies. The idea goes back to the jittery days of the early

Cold War: If a hostile foreign power were to drop a nuke on Washington, the designated survivors would be spared the carnage and could carry on the nation's vital business from there. We were Noah's Ark for the nuclear age, America's last, best, desperate hope, however remote the threat of Armageddon might have been.

Odd as it may sound, the seeds of this book were planted in that bunker. That night was about more than just maintaining continuity of agency operations. It was about preserving the country by safeguarding the key institutions that defend America's values. The Federal Bureau of Investigation (FBI) had done that with excellence for over a century. I had some time that evening to ask myself: *What defines the Bureau and makes it special?* As I reflected—and being locked in a subterranean shelter has a way of focusing the mind, by the way—I did an inventory. I concluded that the FBI maintained its exceptional record of performance not because of its budgets, technology, weapons, or any other external factor, but rather because it had developed and instilled an organizational code that demanded internal excellence at all times, from everyone. This isn't a throwaway line. When I say we held ourselves to the highest standards, it's because I know we policed our internal behavior with the same zeal we famously applied to hunting killers, thieves, and spies. Buildings could be reconstructed, leaders replaced, but what was essential and unchanging about the Bureau was the extraordinary practice of excellence that was instilled in agents from the moment they entered the academy. I call it *The FBI Way*.

I HAD NO IDEA HOW GOOD WE HAD IT BACK THEN IN THE bunker.

In those simpler days, we knew who our enemies were, criminals at home and hostile powers abroad. The world was neatly divided between *us* and *them*. And no one had any doubt who the good guys were . . .

Now look.

We've lived through a period where some senior leaders, even during a global pandemic, caused many Americans to doubt the vital bulwarks of freedom that comprise our federal law enforcement and intelligence communities—the very institutions that have devoted themselves to keeping us safe. Political partisanship and trash talk caused many Americans to wonder which way was up. Who knows how long it might take to restore faith in our institutions? Let me say this as plainly as I know how:

These attacks do not reflect the reality of everyday excellence at those agencies.

When we cast doubt on our most essential institutions, we're doubting the career professionals who come to work every day trying to defend our democracy. This isn't just about me. It's also about my former colleagues at the FBI, the CIA, the National Security Agency, and even the Centers for Disease Control and Prevention and the National Institutes of Health. They are some of the greatest patriots I know, men and women who have spent long careers, often at genuine risk to themselves, defending the rule of law and keeping Americans safe in an often corrupt and volatile world. These heroes get it right most of the time. In fact, the track record of high performance at these agencies surpasses the success rate at the most revered companies, organizations, and teams. That's why it's worth learning how these folks operate.

This book reveals how the FBI does it. In the intelligence, law enforcement, and military world, the term "hot wash" describes an immediate after-action discussion of what went right and wrong following a tactical operation, exercise, or crisis incident. The phrase started with combat soldiers who doused their weapons with hot water to remove dirt and grime until they could properly break down and clean their rifles. Now the concept refers to any team debrief designed to identify lessons learned that can be applied to the next mission. The chapters that follow are the "hot wash" after my career. Feel free to take some or all of what I learned and use it on your journey toward enhanced value-based performance. It's how the FBI can view each of its senior leaders as designated survivors, capable of preserving its values and mission with excellence. And it's how you and your leadership team can do the same. I've condensed the Bureau's process of preserving and protecting its core values into what I call the Seven C's: Code, Conservancy, Clarity,

Consequences, Compassion, Credibility, and Consistency. That's *The FBI Way.*

I'm sharing an insider's perspective on exactly how a treasured national institution really works. In fact, I happen to think that the secret to how the men and women of the Federal Bureau of Investigation successfully perform could work for you, too, no matter your profession or stage of your career.

I spent nearly three decades in the FBI, as a street agent, a program supervisor at FBI Headquarters, a squad supervisor in a field office, and the head of an internal disciplinary unit in the Office of Professional Responsibility (OPR). Later I became the number two official in the Miami Field Office, followed by senior executive roles as an inspector, the Bureau's chief inspector, the special agent in charge of the Cleveland Field Office, and, finally, the assistant director (AD) for counterintelligence. I know the Bureau through and through.

My inside observation perch gave me an opportunity to study patterns of conduct among high-achieving, ethical individuals and draw conclusions about why, when, and how good people sometimes did bad things. I also learned the strengths of the system responsible for maintaining the FBI's historic lack of systemic corruption among a global workforce of more than thirty-five thousand people in over sixty nations. During my time, less than 2 percent of employees were accused of misconduct in any given year, let alone found to have committed any. It's all a matter of perspective.

The FBI isn't perfect. No human organization is. But it is

an honorable and hugely valuable institution whose integrity-based excellence should be explained, studied, and preserved. If you're looking for a book that claims the Bureau has the exclusive answer to integrity, this isn't it. But if you're seeking to learn how the best law enforcement and security agency in the world gets it right most of the time, read on. Join me in this after-action hot wash.

The FBI, like other U.S. intelligence agencies, practices a concept called "Need to Know." The access you are permitted is based on whether you need that data to do your job. I'm sharing the life lessons I've learned inside the Bureau because I believe you need to know something important: Beyond any headlines of the moment, beyond any politically driven attacks, beyond any rare but high-profile fumbles stands one of our nation's most essential institutions. You need to know that this institution is composed of extraordinary humans governed by an equally extraordinary structure designed to preserve the meaning behind the FBI's motto of Fidelity, Bravery, and Integrity. That same internal structure—its workings and the stories of the human beings it impacts—holds important lessons for our own careers, companies, and country. That process, that structure, those values, and the stories that bring them alive are all part of what I call *The FBI Way*. It's a path toward excellence. And now it can be yours.

1

CODE

I WAS A KEEPER OF *THE CODE*—THE FBI'S CODE OF CON-
duct. For portions of my FBI leadership career, my assignment required me to apply the Bureau's code against the
proven misconduct of some of the finest people in our nation—
our own agents. These talented and tenacious public servants
passed the most stringent background investigations and regular reinvestigations, periodic polygraph exams, random drug
tests, and arduous annual financial disclosures. Yet as high as
those individuals' standards were, they sometimes fell short
of the Bureau's standards. That's where I came in.

A code is a system of principles or rules. Companies, communities, and countries all need a code that reflects their values
if those entities, and those values, are to survive and thrive. You
don't need to be in law enforcement, intelligence, or security
work to benefit from the pages that follow. In fact, this book is

meant for people of all walks of life and for any group, large or small. If you adopt the concept of the Seven C's, you can protect and preserve your values, your code, against all threats, internal and external.

Even as a young kid, growing up in a small Connecticut town, I was intrigued by the notion of an elite agency fighting for justice. We lived close enough to New York City that our newspapers and television stations were New York based. I was fascinated by reports of the FBI's takedowns of mob families and crime bosses. The fact that its agents seemed to use brainpower to battle bad guys was an extra bonus. It didn't hurt that the TV crime dramas of the day portrayed FBI agents as heroes who always solved that week's mystery in an hour or less, including commercials.

At age eleven, I handwrote a letter to the head of the FBI field office in New Haven and told him, matter-of-factly, that I wanted to be a special agent. To my amazement, he wrote back with a personalized signed letter that included all the requirements I would have to meet. I think I still have that letter somewhere.

Years later, after becoming the first college graduate in my family, I entered law school. I did well in classes like Contracts, Torts, and the Constitution, but my passion was Criminal Law. I worked for the state public defender's office during my first law school summer. While I gained a deep appreciation for the difficult task of providing a constitutionally guaranteed defense to everyone accused of committing a crime, my heart wasn't in defense work. That fall, I learned from the law school's career office that the FBI had a new initiative. There was an Honors Internship Program that selected a handful of students and paid them to work a summer at FBIHQ in Washington. I submitted my application the next day.

It took the whole school year to get through the background investigation. Since the Bureau viewed the internship as a new recruitment tool, the vetting process was as grueling as it was for a special agent candidate. But I made it. Every morning that summer, I walked into the FBI's hulking headquarters building on Pennsylvania Avenue with its row of American flags flying overhead. Every evening I left the building more convinced than ever that I wanted to be an agent.

My agent application process was in full swing by the time I returned to campus for my last year in law school. Third-year law students, or "3L's," spend a lot of time applying, interviewing, and weighing their employment options. There are also constant questions about who's interviewing with which firm and what salary offers are being made. Many of these discussions are aimed at sizing up your competition. From the reactions I got when I told my classmates about the FBI, it was clear I didn't need to view any of them as rivals.

They couldn't understand why in the world I would want to do something like this. "Are you really going to play cops and robbers?" "How will you live on a government salary?" I told them I'd get by somehow. A few years after I was settled in at the Bureau, my phone started ringing. Some of my former classmates, now fed up with the lack of ethics they saw at their firms or companies, and already tired of the plodding path to a partnership, were asking how they might join the FBI. They were looking to become a part of something bigger, with a better, stronger code.

Learning the Bureau's code started early at the FBI Academy. For me it was day two. There were fifty new agent trainees (yes, we were called NATs) in class 87-16, the numerical identifier for the sixteenth class of 1987. The first day of training was largely administrative, with reams of paperwork, insurance forms, payroll and savings plans decisions, dorm room assignments, a tour of the facility, doling out gear and clothing, and the like. One of the only physical tasks we performed that day was the "trigger-pull test." On day two, several of my classmates were missing. Let me give you the background.

Our issued sidearm was the Smith & Wesson .357 Magnum revolver. The .357 was a hefty mass of steel that was virtually impossible to conceal under a suit unless the observer was blind. Later in my career, the FBI would transition to lightweight semiautomatic pistols. Today's semiautomatic single-action pistols are made with plastic composites, requiring minimal strength to shoot, but the S&W Magnum weighed more than two and a half pounds loaded. And it required at least nine pounds of pressure to pull the trigger.

If you want to get a feel for the trigger-pull test, find a full bottle of wine, grasp it with both hands, and fully extend your arms out in front of you. Hold that position for thirty seconds.

That's the weight of the gun and the length of the test. Next, to get a feel for the pounds of pressure needed to pull the trigger on the .357, grab a full gallon of milk, curl your index finger inside the gallon's handle, and using only the center of your fingertip pad, lift the gallon up off the kitchen counter repeatedly, as many times as you can, for half a minute. Now do the same with the index finger on your weak hand. I'll understand if you want to open that wine bottle after trying.

During initial processing in their local field office, new agent candidates would undergo a battery of exams, including psychological, medical, and fitness. Before they were ever sent to the academy at Quantico, Virginia, the applicants also needed to pass the trigger-pull test to ensure they had what it took to shoot the Magnum. The test required you to "dry fire" an empty weapon by pulling the trigger at least twenty-nine times within thirty seconds with your strong hand, and at least twenty-seven times in thirty seconds with your weak hand. If you couldn't do it, you might be given grip exercises to work on, and your test would be rescheduled, but eventually the local applicant coordinator had to certify that you passed the trigger pull before sending you off to the academy. The rub was, these recruiters were under intense pressure to meet their hiring goals at the time, so trainees began arriving at Quantico without fully passing the strength test.

The unit chief in charge of NATs at the academy was approaching his boiling point over the number of trainees showing up who could not pass the trigger pull once they arrived. We had no idea of this backstory when we walked into class on our second morning and saw six empty seats.

The unit chief later explained he was furious at the field office recruiters who had either been careless with the test results or had not tested their recruits close enough to their departure time to Quantico. He was teaching the recruiters a lesson by withholding credit for hitting their numbers until their candidates could successfully complete a do-over. While this integrity lesson was aimed at agent recruiters, the message to us NATs was equally clear—cutting corners or tweaking results was against the code.

A similar code existed out on the firing range. When I joined in 1987, NATs fired thousands of rounds of ammunition during what most experts believe is the best firearms training in the world. New agents had academics and classroom time at least half the day, every day. The other half of our time alternated between either defensive tactics or firearms training. The opening day on the shooting range was for me, as with many of us, the first time I had fired a handgun. After shooting at the paper targets downrange (and hopefully striking your target and not the one in the next lane), we would hear the voice of God, also known as the lead instructor, loudly over the PA system. Perched high in his covered observation tower, binoculars at the ready, the instructor would announce, "Ensure your weapons are safe, empty, and holstered and move forward to score your targets." It was then we realized we were on an honor system.

Unless we were firing a "course of record," a periodic test

for an official score, it was on us to pull the pen clipped to our shirt, mark a line through each hole in the target, and scrawl our score in large numbers for an instructor to document as he or she walked across the lanes. If your score didn't seem to match the holes in your target, the instructor would recount your calculation. This soon became more frequent as our accuracy improved, and it became harder to distinguish separate and distinct holes when our "groupings" became tighter and tighter. Eventually we started shooting holes through holes and our silhouette targets looked less like they had the measles and more like they were missing an organ. If an instructor believed you had deliberately raised your score, he would issue a warning. If you were foolish enough to again betray the trust placed in you to accurately score your target, you would pack your bags.

The range also taught us a lesson in humility and responsibility. We might all be elite FBI special agent candidates, highly educated, often with advanced degrees and professional experience, but we were still expected to clean up our own mess. By that I mean, when you fired hundreds of rounds of ammo during just one firearms session, you produced hundreds of empty brass shell casings ejected from your weapon throughout the length of the course. These spent casings littered the long asphalt shooting lanes and burrowed into the surrounding grass like loose change fallen on shag carpet. The bits of brass were not only a slip-and-fall hazard as we sprinted from yard line to yard line, but they were also a valuable commodity for the Bureau to sell for scrap metal or reuse. During breaks in the action, the senior instructor would announce over the loudspeaker, "Police up your brass," and we would scramble to retrieve our casings, which while still hot, might have seared into the soft soil.

You could tell a lot about someone by how thoroughly they approached this otherwise meaningless requirement. A shooter who thought the task was both literally and figuratively beneath them, and who might leave many of their casings hiding below the grass blades, would eventually be betrayed by the glint of sudden sunlight off the brass, the resulting flashes silently signaling a poor attitude to the rest of the class. To unknowing passersby, dozens of stooping bucket-wielding figures bobbing in a field to pluck something from the earth might look like farmworkers during crop harvest. But in hindsight, I could see it was all a part of our developing understanding of a Bureau value: sweat the small stuff and get the job done right, or not at all. Whether we realized it or not, the code was working its way into the conscience of the class.

ANYONE SERIOUS ABOUT INTEGRITY NEEDS A CLEAR CODE of conduct. At the FBI, integrity features not only in the Bureau's core values but also in its official motto, "Fidelity, Bravery, Integrity." Unambiguous, well-marked guideposts increase the odds that individual behavior will complement, rather than compromise, core values. If you haven't established basic behavioral benchmarks in your business, organization, team, or family, you should. They don't have to be numerous; in fact, they shouldn't be. Too many rules can very quickly turn into no rules at all. Determine what type of conduct so undermines whatever you or your group stands for that it poses an existential threat. Communicate those "danger zones" clearly and frequently. Whoever it was who said "If you don't stand for something, you might fall for anything" was right on the money.

All good codes of conduct have one common trait: they reflect the core values of an organization. Companies, schools, teams, or any group seeking to codify their rules to live by must first establish core values. The FBI's approach to maintaining its code starts with its eight core values:

- Rigorous obedience to the Constitution of the United States
- Respect for the dignity of all those we protect
- Compassion
- Fairness
- Uncompromising personal integrity and institutional integrity
- Accountability by accepting responsibility for our actions and decisions and the consequences of our actions and decisions
- Leadership, both personal and professional
- Diversity

Typically, the source of our standards is external. They might be handed down from on high, perhaps from our parents or religious figures, a business leader, a coach, or others who influence us. When that's not the case, standards might instead be generated and reinforced from the bottom up, a much more unpredictable integrity model that may not reflect the best interests of the organization. Much later in my career, I was appointed the FBI's chief inspector, responsible for program and performance reviews worldwide. I occasionally observed FBI squads and, at rare times, even entire field offices, where a bad leader enabled an undesirable culture and where eventually, before long, core values were not only abandoned but reset to the lowest common denominator.

Sometimes those leaders, squads, or even offices became toxic, and individuals were removed or reassigned to keep their aberrant values from reaching critical mass. In rare, limited circumstances, I've seen federal agents mistakenly overvalue indictments and convictions to the point they were willing to do or say almost anything to win in court. Those agents didn't last long largely because their peer group, the OPR, or the criminal justice system set them straight and booted them out.

A team, a business, and especially a government can quickly disintegrate when its leader values only the win, not how the win is earned or whether people or values are trampled along the way. Members of such groups have a choice to either reinforce their collective values by pushing back against the leader or to succumb, letting his or her twisted values become theirs.

An organization like the FBI that develops deeply entrenched values and internal enforcement processes is far less likely to see its ethical guardrails demolished, even when those barriers get dented.

In an op-ed in the *New York Times* on May 1, 2019, former FBI director James Comey wrote about the phenomenon of executives whose own codes are tested by a leader who may not have one. Comey observed from his own time around President Donald J. Trump, "Accomplished people lacking inner strength can't resist the compromises necessary to survive Mr. Trump and that adds up to something they will never recover from. It takes character like (former defense secretary) Mattis's to avoid the damage, because Mr. Trump eats your soul in small bites." Comey was talking about having a code, the kind of personal and organizational values needed to survive withering attacks.

The FBI's collective conscience was embodied in its Office of Professional Responsibility. I served as head of OPR's adjudication unit for the eastern half of the United States after initial assignment as a street agent, two years as a counterintelligence supervisor at FBIHQ, and three years supervising squads dedicated to economic espionage and violent crime in San Francisco. In my OPR role and in other more senior leadership assignments, I grappled with often agonizing disciplinary decisions involving serious misconduct allegations against FBI employees in some of the largest field offices in the United States, including New York, Washington, D.C.,

Miami, Newark, Philadelphia, Boston, and others. As an OPR unit chief, I had signature authority for disciplinary decisions from counseling to oral reprimand, letter of censure, suspension without pay, and proposed dismissal. It was never fun. In fact, it was often painful.

In OPR, thick internal misconduct reports queued in my in-box like freight cars waiting to unload their cargo. Each report told the story of an agent, an analyst, a professional specialist, and even a senior executive who went awry, sometimes slightly, occasionally tragically. By the time the completed investigative reports arrived at my desk, my team of adjudicators had attached their analysis of the findings, the related precedent cases, and a recommended disciplinary range. My team's work was almost done, but my decision-making had just started. Often that's when my personal values combined with the Bureau's code to help me make some tough calls.

Most FBI employees entered the Bureau with a strong sense of personal values. Yet, that didn't mean those standards totally aligned with those of their coworkers or the institution. Factors like age, gender, culture, life experience, and even geography sometimes contributed to disparities between how an individual viewed the world and how the Bureau saw it. Companies, organizations, and even families experience dysfunction when the values of individual members don't quite align with those of the greater group and its mission. That's why a team needs a structure and a process to preserve its code and ultimately, its future.

One of the many aspects of Bureau life that preserves reliance on the FBI code is the Bureau's reluctance to assign agents back to their hometowns. It is still a rare event for anyone to be transferred back home right out of the academy. I tried for twenty-five years to get back to Connecticut, but it never happened. This isn't about keeping an agent off-balance. It's about mitigating the risk that an agent might be more influenced by external factors than by the Bureau's internal code. So of course, the Bureau took this Connecticut Yankee and sent me to Atlanta, Georgia, right after training.

Within two weeks of arriving in Atlanta I found myself smack in the middle of a prison insurrection. Cuba's Fidel Castro had packed up his most heinous criminals, put them on boats, and pointed them to the United States. Now, some of them were indefinitely imprisoned at the federal penitentiary in Atlanta, and not at all happy. They staged a bloody riot, took the guards hostage, and set fire to the prison. One prisoner was murdered and two guards were injured. The unrest lasted eleven days. Since this was a federal prison, the FBI led the response, and most important, the hostage negotiations, in Spanish, to save the lives of the guards and end the siege. Where was I, you might ask?

That was me, way up in tower number four. The tower with all the smoke and fire around it overlooking the main yard. The tower where food and drink had to be sent up via a pulley. I was the guy with the binoculars, the radio, and the revolver. I was the sole federal agent up there with two corrections officers. While my official assignment was to radio our intel center about the movements of the riot leaders (when I could see through the smoke), my tougher task was to keep one of the very angry corrections officers from firing his rifle down at the inmate who was leading the riot. The guard's rifle was bigger than my handgun. About every thirty minutes the guard would point his rifle out our tower window and start to squeeze the trigger. I was in my own negotiation stalemate. For eleven days I managed to talk the guard out of an action that could have ensured the death of every hostage. I guess you could say I convinced him that my code made more sense than his, at least for now.

In Atlanta, the starkest contrast between the local culture and the Bureau's code came from the FBI's role as the nation's lead agency for civil rights investigations. We investigated cross burnings and arsons at black churches. During my time, I was assigned to cover a KKK march down the streets of the city. This wasn't 1950, this was the late 1980s and early 1990s. Not long after I arrived, my supervisor handed me a case involving an accusation of excessive use of force by two Georgia state troopers. After I read through the arrest reports and the complaint by the alleged victim, I was ready to conduct witness interviews. That was the first time I, a rookie FBI agent from Connecticut, heard someone use the N-word in conversation with me. This term didn't come from just any witness. It came from the two Georgia state troopers I was investigating for allegedly beating a black man. That's how they referred to him. Not just one trooper, but both troopers, multiple times. It's all in my notes. A different code, a different culture, one might say. When I got home that evening, I told my wife that it was now official: the Bureau had sent us on a journey to another planet.

Civil rights investigations were a specialty in the FBI, and if you worked enough of those cases you might find yourself being called an "expert." It was frustrating work in part because so many allegations never rose to the level of federal prosecution. It was also particularly challenging to work excessive force cases against the police when the FBI partners with police departments every day. So when an allegation was filed against a senior detective who was running for county sheriff near Athens, Georgia, the only two agents in the small FBI office there knew they needed to call Atlanta. That's what people with ethics do. They recuse themselves to avoid any appearance of conflict while still preserving the mission. That's how I got a road trip to Athens.

Sometimes police officers and even FBI agents try to take the law into their own hands. That's bad, even illegal. But the man who would become sheriff of Oconee County didn't just take the law into his own hands, he surrendered it to someone else. A local business was burglarized. Two sheriff's investigators confronted a suspect, brought him in for questioning, and planted him in an interrogation room with no windows or phone. The business owner was a friend of one of the investigators. After unsuccessfully questioning the suspect, the investigators left the room and returned with the business owner. That's when things went south.

While the investigators continued their interrogation, the business owner beat the suspect. The owner repeatedly struck the guy, knocked his head against the wall, and threatened to kill him. The suspect begged the investigators to stop this. The suspect, now a victim, ended up with a ruptured eardrum, a swollen and bruised eye, and knots on his head. Eventually the investigators drove the victim to his friend's house. He then headed for the hospital emergency room, where the attending doctor confirmed the injuries were consistent with a beating. The next day the victim limped his way to the little FBI resident agency above the post office in Athens. The agents photographed his bruises, took a statement, and made sure the victim had received medical care. The Bureau's civil rights mission wasn't just about enforcing a code, it was about preserving the rule of law. The same law those sheriff's investigators took an oath to uphold. The same oath the vast majority of law enforcement officers are willing to die for.

In the middle of all this, the senior investigator continued his run for sheriff. Amazingly, before we could indict and arrest him, he won. Since the newly minted sheriff was popular enough to win an election, we were concerned about whether the jurors at his trial might simply see his actions as a form of "good old boy" justice. But the solid citizens of Oconee County, Georgia, had a higher code, even if their sheriff didn't.

On December 9, 1988, the new sheriff, his investigator, and the business owner were each federally indicted for conspiracy to violate the victim's rights while in custody and for aiding and abetting the violation of his rights. All three were eventually convicted of civil rights violations. In many states, when a law enforcement officer is convicted of certain federal felonies, he can't wear a badge again. That's what happened to the sheriff. He was convicted and sentenced to prison, where he would spend some time with other folks like him who lived by a degraded code or no code at all.

Unlike my experience with local police misconduct, only a fraction of FBI employee discipline cases involved a total failure to grasp the concept of code. That was mostly because of the incredible investment the Bureau made both in training and in meticulous background investigations before allowing anyone in the door. These yearlong deep dives into the lives of applicants reflected the principle of *Caveat Emptor*, or "Buyer Beware." We wanted to know precisely what we were getting before we bought it. Exhaustive screening measures, including psychological testing, panel interviews, medical exams, and polygraph tests all contributed to keeping the number of FBI employees who might later be accused of misconduct to an absolute minimum.

Once a job candidate successfully passed written exams and a panel interview, the Bureau launched their famous background inquiry. "Full field" investigations, as they're called, tapped into the resources of each of the fifty-six FBI field offices in the United States and the now sixty-three FBI legal attaché (legat) offices abroad. If you grew up in the small town of New Fairfield, as I did, the local constable's office and the resident state trooper would get a visit from a New Haven–based FBI agent who would pull any file involving you or your family. High school records and grades were verified, and former neighbors, bosses, roommates, and significant others were identified and interviewed. If someone had a problem with you, the FBI wanted to know why.

Standard questions included: "Would you trust this person with national security information?" "How about with a gun and a badge?" "How would you describe their temperament, their judgment, their reputation, their loyalty to the country?" "Are they living within their financial means?" Agents visited your college campus, wherever it was, and reviewed disciplinary reports, transcripts, and any delinquent tuition payments. If you ever lived or studied abroad, which is an increasingly common scenario, a lead would be sent to the appropriate legat office in the nearest U.S. embassy or consulate. That legat would enlist the help of the national or local police to check records and conduct interviews.

As was true during my application process, today if an applicant makes it past the full-field investigation, it is time for a polygraph exam. FBI polygraph examiners are the best in the world, not only because of their extensive technical training but because they must have years of experience as an agent before becoming a polygraphist. That means two things—they understand people, and they understand how to conduct an interview. The prepolygraph interview by the examiner is where the questions are reviewed with the candidate and where things suddenly get quite real. For some applicants, this is the first time they ever really confront the difference between their own self-image, their public persona, and reality.

Once the future fed is seated in the polygraph chair, the examiner clearly goes over the upcoming questions and asks if answering those questions will present any issues. For example, if the examiner says, "I'll be asking you if you've ever stolen anything," this is the candidate's chance to share that five years ago they took a box of pencils home from work and they still feel terrible about it. An honest response to the prepolygraph discussion is by far the best approach and, absent a confession to a felony, goes a long way toward successful results. Yet, repeatedly, candidates choose to lie before, during, and after their exams even about things that wouldn't end the process. Drug use is still the issue most lied about on applicant polygraphs, even though past drug use is not an automatic disqualifier. Rather, many people, even those with a strong personal code, seem unable to get beyond the person they think they are and honestly see the person they really are. When the vetting process identifies those people, they don't make it into the FBI.

I would argue the FBI invests far more effort in selecting its employees than the nation does in choosing its presidents.

While the FBI protects our democracy, it doesn't have to practice it when picking who it employs. The hiring process is grueling and unforgiving because the goal, not always achieved, is to find the people with the highest standards. One of my earliest supervisors in the Bureau was a particularly disciplined and decent human being. When we would hear a rare account of an FBI employee being escorted out of some field office for some ridiculously low-level fraud or embezzlement, he would turn to me and say, "If you ever see me dragged out in handcuffs, it will be for at least a million dollars." Back then, a million dollars was worth even more than today and would have been impossible to embezzle from the Bureau. What he meant was that the FBI didn't try to hire perfect people, just people whose moral threshold was so high they would likely never have to confront that threshold.

That doesn't mean people don't have breaking points; everyone does. But breaking points can be reset and reinforced through processes and policies. Breaking points can also be avoided or at least delayed through warning signs and accountability. An organization, even a nation, needs established alarm bells to ring when there's a danger of breaching a breaking point. But warnings are not enough. Governance and accountability mechanisms must be agreed upon and maintained for an institution, a company, or even a government to survive.

In fact, the Bureau has better mechanisms to hire new employees than the nation has to pick a president. When President

Trump was referred to as "Individual 1" in a criminal indictment, people started asking me if background investigations were conducted on presidential candidates or even on members of Congress. After all, presidents and congressional members get security clearances. Yet the answer is no. The reason is tied to our national values as a democracy. Rightfully, Americans place high value on the freedom to choose whoever they want as their next congressional member or their next president. We are proud of the notion that anyone can rise to the highest office if they simply win an election. But imagine we imposed some type of barrier to the Oval Office in the form of a full-field background investigation. Imagine if that background investigation identified concerns that precluded the nominee from being granted a "Top Secret" clearance. At that point, a bunch of bureaucrats, not the American voters, would decide who could or could not become president. No one really wants that.

I've had a front-row seat to how this kind of thing works, and doesn't work, when it comes to members of Congress and even a candidate for president. There are limits to what the FBI can and can't do when it comes to someone who, because of a national security concern, either shouldn't run for office or shouldn't continue to hold office. Mostly it's the voters, who likely aren't privy to the classified details, who must read the tea leaves and decide if they want to drink what a candidate is serving. Here's what I mean.

During my career, I've sat across the table from a second-tier presidential candidate and provided what's called a defensive briefing. This one was more like a warning. The candidate didn't have a security clearance, and their motivations were unclear, so I couldn't share with them all the details of how we knew that they were actively and knowingly involved with foreign intelligence officers. But I could sure as hell let the candidate know that whatever their good-faith reason was for engaging with these people, the foreigners had a plan of their own. The candidate warily thanked me for the briefing. I think they got the message, even if it was one they didn't want to hear. This candidate's run for the White House was short-lived, but what if it had lasted? What if their foreign contacts got the upper hand? What if this candidate had won the election?

I had a similar sit-down with a member of Congress. This time the conversation was less subtle. I told the representative that a foreign intelligence service considered the congressional member to be their asset. A recruited source. A snitch. I'm not allowed to share this official's response, except to tell you that I wasn't buying any of it. We ended our tense discussion with the understanding that one of us needed to stop what they were doing, and it wasn't going to be me. This member is no longer in Congress, but what if they were, what if they hadn't stopped?

In the case of both the presidential candidate and the congressperson, the FBI would have opened counterintelligence cases to try and determine whether those people were targeted, vulnerable, or already playing for another team. We would have taken the least intrusive approach to avoid knocking on doors, conducting overt interviews, and briefing too many politicians who might leak it as fast as they could speed-dial CNN. That's because that kind of bull-in-a-china-shop method would quickly lead to accusations that the FBI was a deep-state cabal trying to take down an elected official. Of course, taking a quieter approach, like using human sources and probing staff members, would also risk inevitable accusations that the Bureau was abusing its authority, spying on a campaign, or had its own political bias. That's why the FBI often finds itself between a rock and a hard place even when it is trying to do what's best for the nation's security. That's precisely what happened during the 2016 presidential campaign.

Voters used to be better equipped to figure out which candidate was least likely to endanger us, if that concern ever even came up. There has previously been a kind of national vetting process that occurs in the lengthy lead-up to an election where media scrutiny, caucuses, public debates, speeches, and platforms are supposed to help us gain a deep understanding of a candidate. Or at least as deep an understanding as can be gained when, as in 2016, the candidate was a private businessman who never held public office. For Americans, the value we have placed on our democratic principles and on free, unfettered elections has overridden the risk of not more formally vetting our candidates. In the past, we trusted that an unworthy candidate wouldn't make it past an election, or if he did, that he wouldn't make it past his first term. It's not foolproof.

It doesn't work when our code is different from the candidate's code.

If we later discovered that our trust was mistaken, our system could attempt to remove a president through impeachment, but that process was subject to highly political factors. Now the world has become a far more complex place filled with social media propaganda, computer hacking, and foreign nations secretly interfering with our elections. Truth is fiction, up is down, black is white. Voters need to be far more sophisticated just to keep up. Just to ensure the candidate's code is consistent with ours.

Some of the highest-ranking people in our government may never be subjected to the same vetting required for even seemingly routine FBI jobs—say, for a Bureau auto mechanic or administrative assistant. That was the case during the controversial and highly contentious confirmation process for Supreme Court Justice Brett Kavanaugh. When new and multiple concerns over sexual misconduct, alcohol abuse, and temperament arose, the White House blocked the FBI from conducting a second full-field investigation of Kavanaugh. The president's advisers and GOP senators asserted that since Kavanaugh was already a sitting federal appellate court judge, he had already survived background investigations. They had little interest in fleshing out the new allegations. Not only was a polygraph never done, but the White House dictated the limited parameters of what the Bureau could and could not dig into.

This kind of "cover-up in plain sight" was permissible

because of our established policy that treats any agency requesting an FBI background investigation or reinvestigation as a business client. Since the White House is the requesting agency for a Supreme Court nominee, it is a "client" who can dictate the parameters of the reinvestigation. In contrast, when the FBI investigates its own job candidates, or for that matter, anything else, the goal is the truth, and the client is the American people. The current policy on backgrounds and reinvestigations for high-level roles needs to change if we're going to avoid abuse of power. No policy should simply trust the White House, Congress, or any requesting agency to do the right thing when it comes to vetting their own nominees.

It wasn't always like this. When I was AD for counterintelligence (CI), I had my turn at dealing with potentially serious national security and judgment concerns about a presidential nominee for a very important office. The issue for this nominee came up during an FBI investigation and it couldn't be ignored. In fact, we knew the president would be livid if we didn't raise the concerns. So, along with the head of the Bureau's National Security Branch, I hopped in a car and headed to our requested appointment with a top presidential adviser in the White House situation room. We needed to raise a question about code.

It was never good news when the Bureau's AD for CI requested a meeting, and the adviser knew something was wrong. But here's the thing; once the White House was fully briefed and we presented a recommended course of action, the only guidance we got was to get to the truth as quickly as possible. In fact, the White House must have told this nominee to get with the program, because they agreed to a polygraph and an interview that helped mitigate our concerns. In this case, the FBI, the White House, and the nominee shared the same code of conduct and values, to the benefit of our nation's security. That code was the United States Constitution. But what if that wasn't the case? What if perhaps the FBI answered to an attorney general who saw things differently, maybe had his own code? And what if, just maybe, we had a president who had no code at all?

To FBI employees, code isn't just a concept of what goes on inside the Bureau and among its people. Rather, it's literally what the FBI does for a living—it enforces the U.S. criminal code, over three hundred federal laws, from the little-known Migratory Bird Act and the National Refrigerator Act, to more high-profile statutes related to civil rights, cybercrime, public corruption, bank robbery, kidnapping, extortion, fraud, drugs, organized crime, espionage, and terrorism. Maybe since the FBI is in the code enforcement business, it's easier for its employees to internalize the Bureau's own standards and to try to live up to them every day.

During my time in the FBI, the Bureau's counterintelligence professionals knew all about the importance of preserving their values. When you mentioned "code" to one of these spy catchers, they immediately thought of the encryption methods used by their targets to send messages between officers, embassies, and operatives. They knew that breaking an adversary's code was the ultimate win and that the only way to do that was to learn the "key" that decrypts the code. Back then, that meant the most targeted person inside a foreign embassy or consulate might not be the ambassador, the senior intelligence officer, or the military attaché—it might be the code clerk, if you could even find him. A hostile nation's code clerk, posted to the United States, lived the life of a hermit. He didn't go out much, certainly not alone, and often while under surveillance by his own people. Figuring out who had access to the code was step one. Step two was trying to recruit him. Step three was supposed to be celebration, unless, of course, there was a murder involved.

My Atlanta squad supervisor called me into his office one day and closed the door. He was giving me a "drop everything" scorcher out of Washington. There was no paper or file number yet, just a secure phone call from FBIHQ to my boss. Apparently, the county police in an Atlanta suburb had discovered a corpse in an apartment. Somewhere in the apartment they found the business card of a Washington, D.C.–based FBI agent. The cops' phone call to that agent prompted all hell to break loose in the nation's capital. Now Washington was sharing the love with us.

First, I got hold of the Washington Field Office agent whose business card was found in the apartment. On a secure line, he explained that the FBI had recruited a code clerk from a certain country. The guy was playing for our team until he disappeared.

The Bureau had been frantically searching for this critical asset for several days. To make things worse, we knew we weren't the only ones looking for him. His own country had no idea where their code clerk was and had dispatched a "search" squad from back home to find him. We were in a race against an adversary that wouldn't hesitate to kill. In fact, with the report of a dead body outside Atlanta, they might have already done it.

I called the assigned homicide detective, introduced myself, and asked if I could pay a visit. His department worked closely with my FBI colleagues on the violent crime squad and he was eager for any information that might help solve his murder investigation. So was I. On that call, I learned that the dead body belonged to a woman. Our asset was male. Now I really wanted to assess the crime scene. But my supervisor stopped me as I was about to race out of the office. He said that Oliver "Buck" Revell, an FBI executive assistant director (EAD), wanted me to call him on the secure phone. Revell, now a Bureau legend, was one of the "holy trinity," one of the top three officials under the director. Mr. Revell had control of all FBI investigations, while I was a lowly field agent. This kind of phone call simply did not happen. I asked my boss if he was joking; he shook his head, shrugged his shoulders, and handed me Revell's number.

As best as I can recall, here's how the call went down:

"This is Buck Revell."

"Yes, sir. This is Frank Figliuzzi in Atlanta."

"Frank, I want you to understand how serious this is. We

may have had an act of international terrorism in Atlanta, Georgia."

"Yes, sir."

"We think a hit team is already here and that they murdered our asset's wife in Georgia. They might have already murdered our source somewhere, too. I need you to tell me what the hell happened down there. Have you been to the police yet?"

"No, sir, I was just headed there."

"Well, get on it."

A table full of detectives awaited me at the police department. The first thing I did was apologize. I explained that I didn't know much and that some of what I knew was classified. But I did share that we'd really like to find the victim's husband. I provided his name and photo, told them the husband was a foreign embassy employee based in Washington, and said he was now missing. I also explained that there was some concern that this murder might have been committed by professionals, maybe even a team of them. The detectives knew the score; they seemed to understand what was happening. They briefed me on everything they had. There were interviews of neighbors and coworkers, items found in the apartment, accounts of loud noise and yelling, a door slamming. It looked like the deceased had been staying at this place during some company-related training or temporary assignment. I wanted to see the crime scene photos.

This was no professional hit. The body was placed flat on her back, fully clothed, in the center of the room. She was covered with a blanket neatly tucked around her form. A handwritten note in her native language was pinned atop the blanket. Even before we translated the note, I knew the person who did this cared about the woman, maybe even loved her. Once translated, the note confirmed there was both love and regret. I had seen enough to figure it was more likely than not that the FBI asset had murdered his wife and was now on the run. The only remaining question was who would find him first.

We lost the race. There was indeed a team of bad guys looking for our guy, or should I say, their guy. The code clerk had made the awful decision to return to Washington. We learned that he had contact with his embassy. He wanted back in. His colleagues apparently convinced him to stay put; they would send friends to pick him up. The folks who grabbed him off that street corner were not his friends. Bureau agents raced to find him, intercept his captors, scour the airports, and scroll through flight manifests. It was too late; he was gone.

After the sequence was all pieced together, the correct airline flight figured out, the special "escorts" identified, airline employees interviewed, and airport security video analyzed, the picture became clearer. The code clerk was likely drugged, dragged through the airport, presented to the gate agent with a false passport, and dropped into his seat by his newfound buddies. He slept the entire way home. Once back in his country, his government's executioners ensured that their code clerk would sleep forever. The clerk had tried to live by a new code but couldn't escape the deadly confines of his old one.

You can't live by two codes at once. You also can't spot and avoid the kinds of codes and conduct that threaten your values if you never even develop a strong sense of what it is that you value. You'll never see the threat coming. The foreign code clerk tried to straddle two codes of conduct, and it ended up getting him killed. We might not die from an absence of code, but regardless of who we are, our lives and livelihoods are enhanced when we know what we stand for. It may seem counterintuitive, but codes of conduct aren't confining. Living by a code lowers the risk of falling victim to bad decisions, bad people, and bad outcomes.

2

CONSERVANCY

W HEN YOU ENTER THE FBI, YOU JOIN A CONSERVANCY. Conservancy is a collective effort to preserve and protect the true worth of a place or thing. People in a conservancy agree to become stewards accountable for sustaining an entity greater than themselves. When members of a group begin to view themselves as accountable stewards, they don't just tolerate the group's values, they assimilate those values. An organization starts to sow the seeds of stewardship by holding its members accountable for how their conduct impacts the greater group.

In the Bureau, everyone is accountable to someone. Field agents answer to their squad supervisors, who answer to assistant special agents in charge (ASACs), who answer to special agents in charge (SACs), who answer to the deputy director, who answers to the director, who answers to the deputy attorney general, who answers to the attorney general of the United States. Ultimately, we all answered to the American people through their elected representatives in Congress. And members of Congress had to answer to their constituents back home.

Leadership accountability is vital to preservation of a group's values. The conduct of the most senior leaders, and their stance toward misconduct, ultimately drive the integrity of the group. Assistant directors at FBIHQ ran each of the operational, support, and administrative programs in the FBI and briefed executive assistant directors and the director at least every weekday. Following those morning briefings, the director would brief the attorney general and then the two of them, in those days, would head off to the White House to brief the president. And not a day went by when one of us wasn't on the Hill briefing one of the Senate or House committees. In OPR, we knew the DOJ inspector general (IG) had visibility into each one of our cases and could pluck a particularly significant internal allegation from our in-box at any time. This system of accountability and oversight worked well, but only because everyone acknowledged that we all answered to someone.

The conservancy concept, when correctly executed, is a powerful way to maintain organizational standards. In the Bureau, this concept isn't limited to just the senior executives; it was part of the fabric of the FBI's compliance mechanisms. Almost every agent will tell you that early in their career they were tapped on the shoulder by their squad supervisor and handed a "new case." This new assignment turned out to be an investigation of the latest Bureau car (bucar) fender bender involving a squad mate. When minor accidents occurred with Bureau vehicles, tradition was that the mandatory accident inquiry be conducted by whoever had had the immediately preceding accident. If no one could recall who that person was (a mysteriously frequent phenomenon), the task would go to the newest agent on the squad.

These accident inquiries were the real deal. You couldn't just look the other way if a fellow agent was at fault. A comprehensive government report was required to include photographs, interviews of other parties, a written statement by the agent driver, a sketch of the accident scene, and a conclusion as to what happened. Your supervisor would review your work and kick it back if it didn't pass muster. This was the last thing you needed on top of an already exhaustive caseload. But the dual message was clear: "We're all accountable to one another," and "When one of us screws up, it impacts the rest of us."

This notion of collective conservancy extended throughout the Bureau, including how we staffed OPR. An agent entering the management ranks and needing to fulfill their mandatory time somewhere at FBIHQ in Washington could seek a supervisory position in an OPR investigative or adjudicative unit. Higher-level management and executive positions in OPR were available as your career advanced. Many agents understandably eschewed the unpleasant work of OPR and instead chose operational programs in the counterterrorism, counterintelligence, cyber, or criminal divisions. Yet others made a conscious decision to pull at least one management tour immersed in the sensitive internal work they knew would make them more well-rounded leaders. My own brief stints in the Bureau's internal functions proved invaluable in my later leadership roles.

Even if you did not raise your hand for formal assignment to OPR in Washington, an aspiring leader couldn't avoid conducting an internal inquiry. The OPR staff at FBIHQ could not possibly address every infraction allegation, nor was that how the system was designed. If you were a field supervisor, perhaps running an organized crime squad in Chicago, you were still expected to contribute to this component of the conservancy. Your turn would come whenever OPR deemed an allegation in your office suitable to delegate to the field. While you would never be assigned an inquiry related to your own team, you would certainly be tapped to examine an allegation within the same field office. In delegated matters, the head of the office would review your investigative findings and issue a disciplinary decision. I learned that holding one another accountable was an ever-present element of FBI leadership.

Similarly, climbing the Bureau's career ladder required that you participate in a specified number of inspections. The FBI's Inspection Division was the equivalent of a professional traveling audit staff found in many large corporations. As with OPR inquiries, you could choose to conduct inspections full-time while based at FBIHQ or you could complete the requisite audits periodically from your current assignment. Either way, throughout your leadership journey, you would find yourself as both the inspector and the inspected.

No program or office was exempt from inspection, which generally occurred at least every three years. During my career, I participated in inspections of over a dozen field offices; of a few headquarters divisions; and of legal attaché offices in London, Tel Aviv, and Amman, as well as in reviews of several agent-involved shootings. To learn as much as I could about every corner and crevice of the Bureau, I became one of only nine full-time inspectors within the FBI's Senior Executive Service. This meant that I led traveling teams of assistant inspectors virtually nonstop for one year. At the end of that year, I was appointed the FBI's chief inspector by then director Robert Mueller. My time away from operational work in Counterintelligence, Counterterrorism, White-Collar Crime, and Civil Rights represented a fraction of my career. But it turned out to be a much greater percentage of my education concerning how those programs, and the FBI, functioned.

The Bureau's inspection process was legendary for its depth and breadth. Inspectors had to make "calls" on the efficiency and effectiveness of each squad, each program, and each leader in the Bureau. Large teams from all over the FBI would descend upon an office for two or three weeks. Investigative and informant files were pulled and reviewed, priorities and results assessed in relation to the local crime problems and national security threats. Supervisors and agents were interviewed and external partners in local, county, state, and federal law enforcement were asked how the FBI was doing and what it could do better. If particular "best practices" were identified, they were published and shared with other offices.

This was far more than a numbers game. A high volume of arrests might mean that the office leadership was choosing "quick hit" statistics over meaningful, complex investigations. One core question was at the heart of each inspection: "What impact is this office and its leaders having on this community?" The head of any organization determines how seriously compliance is taken, and the FBI is no exception. I personally briefed Director Mueller on the findings of each inspection. Thereafter, a video conference was scheduled with the head of the inspected office so the director could review key results with that leader. Even in the days before high-definition video, beads of sweat were still visible on the foreheads of SACs as they explained themselves.

I'm convinced the FBI's practice of mandatory leadership participation in both the OPR and inspection processes forges more knowledgeable and accountable leaders. Many companies unconsciously send the message to their employees that compliance and ethics is someone else's job. Corporations often make audit staff assignments optional for executive trainees or fail to properly incentivize or reward such roles. When it comes to addressing allegations of misconduct, most companies allocate that responsibility solely to human resources or legal departments. Yet, how can you trust your leaders to comply with standards if you don't trust them to enforce those standards?

THE FBI ESTABLISHED A SENIOR EXECUTIVE SERVICE (SES) disciplinary board to hold its top tier of leaders accountable when accused of misconduct. While SAC of the Cleveland Division, I was named to this board and periodically traveled to Washington when the group was convened to make disciplinary decisions. While some FBI employees may have perceived the existence of a separate executive disciplinary board as favoritism, the truth was quite the opposite. Appointment into the government-wide SES was considered the pinnacle of an FBI management career. The SES rank came with a different salary structure, better retirement benefits, and the potential for enhanced bonuses. But for the senior executive found guilty of misconduct, the penalties could be severe. The higher your role as a conservator, the more accountable you became.

The U.S. Office of Personnel Management (OPM) deemed that an SES member could not be suspended without pay for less than fourteen days. While this rule may have made other agencies reluctant to issue any suspensions, in the FBI, this meant infractions that might have resulted in a few days off for nonexecutives resulted in a minimum loss of half a month's salary for executives. Significantly, it was rare for the SES disciplinary board to recommend suspensions greater than fourteen days. Again, this wasn't because executives were looking out for one another. Rather, the thinking was that if one of us, who was supposed be a conservator of Bureau standards, did something meriting more than fourteen days of suspension, that person didn't deserve to remain among us. Those folks were either demoted from the SES or terminated.

THINGS CAN QUICKLY GO SOUTH WHEN A SENIOR LEADER unilaterally decides they are somehow less accountable. For example, many Americans understandably assert that President Trump veered well outside his executive branch lane to challenge the principle of three equal branches of government. His refusal to acknowledge congressional subpoenas and his apparent disregard for the rule of law, evidenced in his disdain for the FBI and the Department of Justice, have tested our national values and even our democratic form of government. Yet certain FBI leaders made it easier for Trump to challenge the system when they wittingly or unwittingly strayed from the Bureau's well-established standards and accountability. The questionable judgment of those officials sparked public mistrust of the Bureau and fueled the president's repeated efforts to fan those flames of doubt. James Comey unwittingly fell into that role.

A MAN OF UNCOMPROMISING INTEGRITY OFTEN DESCRIBED as the antithesis of President Trump, Jim Comey was appointed

FBI director by President Barack Obama and served until he was fired by Trump in 2017. The role of FBI director is not a cabinet-level position. Rather, the director answers to the deputy attorney general (DAG) and ultimately to the attorney general. Importantly, we can't discuss Comey's judgment and decision-making during the tumultuous lead-up to his termination without understanding the contrast between his previous government positions and his post at the FBI. Eight years before becoming director, Comey served as the DAG for almost two years under President George W. Bush. Prior to becoming the DAG, Comey served for two years as the U.S. Attorney (USA) for the Southern District of New York. That meant that before ever becoming FBI director, Comey already held two of the most powerful positions in the Department of Justice.

AS THE USA IN NEW YORK, COMEY LED MANY OF THE MOST significant federal prosecutions in the nation, and as the DAG, he made "the buck stops here" decisions on the most complex operational challenges for the entire Justice Department, including the FBI and its director. Comey's seasoned experience as a top prosecutive shot-caller likely served him well as FBI director—until one day he forgot which job he held and to whom he was accountable.

There's no need to dive deeply into the well-worn story. Most of us know that Comey held a dramatic press conference at FBIHQ on July 5, 2016, to announce he was not recommending charges be brought by the DOJ against Hillary Clinton for her mishandling of classified data. Here's the problem: it's not the FBI's job to decide who gets prosecuted. That's why we have prosecutors. In fact, in a big building marked "Department of Justice" just across the street from FBI Headquarters, there are hundreds of career prosecutors, including the one who was Comey's boss, the attorney general of the United States. When I was head of the FBI in northern Ohio, I would have been summarily removed if I called a press conference after a high-profile investigation of a public figure to announce, as Comey did, that "no reasonable prosecutor would bring such a case." SACs of field offices are often referred to as "kings of their domains," but we were all accountable to someone. In the FBI, if the rules apply to an employee in Cleveland, they are supposed to apply to everyone, even the director.

Comey then compounded the Bureau's image problems on October 28, 2016. He felt compelled to notify congressional oversight committees that the FBI had reopened the investigation into Clinton's handling of classified data because of newly discovered "Emails that appear to be pertinent to the investigation." Again, Comey did not need to drag the Bureau into Act II of an already dramatic production. The Bureau's computer forensics analysts were quite capable of applying customized filters to a hard drive to quickly determine whether it contained any previously unknown emails. Comey could have waited for this analysis and then simply told Congress the results. Instead, once again, because of a good-faith effort to do what he deemed was right, Comey caused the public to perceive the FBI as political.

Then, just nine days later, on the eve of the presidential election, Comey had no choice but to inform Congress of the Bureau's finding that virtually all the newly found emails were duplicates of what the FBI already had. But the damage to the Bureau's public perception was done. And the following year, as the cloud of Russia's interference in the 2016 election consumed the Trump administration, Comey's well-intentioned missteps handed President Trump the excuse he needed to rid himself of an FBI director he perceived as a direct threat.

Comey's actions were akin to a museum conservator who spots some smoke and douses the entire art collection with water instead of removing the precious artwork from the building. The damage to the most valuable holdings could have been prevented by a more judicious and strategic response. Comey's damage to the public perception of the Bureau could have been avoided if he had thought about the second- and third-order consequences and just kept the FBI out of the decision on whether to prosecute Clinton. What happened to Comey could happen to any conservator who falls into the trap of thinking no one else can be trusted with saving the valuables. That lapse can make us overreact and cause greater damage to what we're trying to save. But if we view our entire team as conservators and focus on protecting them instead of ourselves, we're more likely to preserve what's important.

IT'S EASIER TO SEE HOW THE BUREAU VIEWS ITS EMPLOYEES as conservators of the agency's core values if you more broadly consider the FBI as conservator of our national values. Every FBI employee raises their right hand and takes the same oath of office that I took my first day at the academy alongside my fifty classmates in the new agent trainee (NAT) class 87-16:

"I, Frank Figliuzzi, do solemnly swear (or affirm) that I will support and defend the constitution of the United States against all enemies, foreign and domestic; that I will bear true faith and allegiance to the same; that I take this obligation freely, without any mental reservation or purpose of evasion; and that I will well and faithfully discharge the duties of the office on which I am about to enter. So help me God."

We repeated the oath on the last day of training during our graduation ceremony, in front of our family, our friends, our instructors, and the FBI director. In my class, our elected class leader delivered a brief speech, containing comic references only his fellow training survivors would understand. Fifty of us had started this journey but only thirty-nine remained on graduation day. Most of those who didn't make it had showed up unprepared for the physical demands of training and were permitted to "roll back" into a subsequent class once they could prove their fitness. One classmate packed up and left after our first day on the firing range. We were told that he never fully contemplated having to take a life until he squared off in front of the standard silhouette target and squeezed the trigger.

On graduation day, an official photo was taken as the director handed each of us our badge and credentials, and everyone adjourned to a simple reception where we started becoming reacquainted with our loved ones. The happy occasion was tempered by the venue for the festivities—the academy's Hall of Honor, where a memorial wall displays the names and images of the FBI's service martyrs who lost their lives in the line of duty. As trainees, we had passed that wall every day, but on this day, the memorial took on added significance.

In case we needed any further reminder of the dangers awaiting us, our hands had been previously inked and printed in case our remains needed to be identified or our presence at a scene confirmed. Bullets fired through the barrels of our issued weapons were collected and preserved to document the rifling mark unique to each of our guns. In one class, our instructor advised that the latest statistics indicated at least one of us would fire our weapons at an adversary within six months. Our last act before departing the Quantico campus was to report to the gunsmith, who handed each of us our sidearm. Locked and loaded, we headed off campus and into the public arena for the first time as special agents.

Our months of intense law enforcement and intelligence immersion included: criminal procedure; statutory elements of hundreds of federal laws enforced by the FBI; civil rights; terrorism; espionage; organized crime; white-collar crime; violent crime; interview techniques; informant development; crime scene analysis; fingerprinting; surveillance exercises in the nearby town; thousands of rounds of ammunition fired indoors, outdoors, in daylight and darkness; defensive tactics; investigative and arrest modules with professional actors in the mock town called Hogan's Alley; obstacle courses; endless rounds of boxing; CPR certification; surviving pepper spray; running miles on roads, tracks and forest trails; performing thousands of push-ups and sit-ups; diving feetfirst, ankles crossed, head to chest, from the high-dive board into the pool to simulate leaping from a distressed surveillance aircraft; and being locked in a cage with one partner and one "bad guy" until someone was handcuffed (preferably the bad guy). We were ready to defend the nation and ourselves. Our roles as conservators of the Constitution had just begun.

CONSERVANCY DEMANDS SACRIFICE. YOU CAN'T HEED THE call of conservancy without sacrificing precious time, energy, sleep, family life, health, and sometimes even your life. By the time an FBI agent completes their career, countless holidays, vacations, birthdays, and anniversaries are missed or interrupted, never to be reclaimed. After the academy, my career progression took me from my home in Connecticut to assignments in: Atlanta; Washington, D.C.; San Francisco; Washington again; Miami; once more to Washington; Cleveland; and finally back to Washington, D.C., as an assistant director. For two of those Washington assignments, we made a family decision that I would go alone and commute back home on weekends. For example, we knew that my assignment as inspector required near constant travel and would last no more than a year or two, so my family happily remained in sunny Florida. Later, when I was promoted to assistant director, my wife, a respected nurse educator, stayed back in Cleveland. Our youngest son made us promise that he would do all four years of high school in one place, and he needed to complete his senior year. He had watched as we moved his older brother in the middle of high school and wanted no part of that.

Somehow, despite the potentially negative impact of cross-country moves, our two sons managed to become decent, smart, and caring adults with careers dedicated to helping others. Much of the credit for that goes to my wife. The FBI interviews your spouse or significant other as part of the application process. Back then, we were young with no kids and ready for adventure. A female agent visited our apartment and met alone with my wife. The agent repeatedly explained to her that we could and would be transferred anywhere based on the "needs of the Bureau," and that there would be many nights when I simply would not be around. The agent was looking for acknowledgment that the special agent role was a vocation, not merely another career. Even though my wife could not possibly know everything she was signing up for, she was thankfully "all in." Soon after I earned the title special agent, my wife started jokingly referring to herself as a special spouse; she couldn't have been more accurate. Families need conservators; she was ours.

THE SACRIFICES OF A COMMITTED CONSERVATOR CAN GO well beyond missed weekends and family inconveniences. Sometimes you sacrifice corners of your psyche. Like many who spend a career in law enforcement, I'm sometimes asked to describe the most disturbing thing I've ever seen. Can I give you some advice? Don't ask cops, rescue workers, or combat veterans to do this. It's one thing for professionals to discuss such stories among themselves or with their loved ones; it might even be a form of therapy. But when unsuspecting civilians pose this question, they're asking you to relive the unimaginable and share it with someone who likely isn't ready for the answer. In fact, I'll understand if you want to skip the next few paragraphs that illustrate the indelible impact on an individual who served as a conservator of the public's safety.

I've encountered my share of murdered, decomposing bodies, including one that was literally melting like wax under the summer sun in an Ohio field, the remnant of a drug deal gone bad. I've also supervised a Crimes Against Children squad in San Francisco. I'm still haunted by images of exploited kids, including the five-year-old boy knocked out with chloroform, molested, then beaten with a curtain rod in an unsuccessful attempt to awaken him, and finally wrapped in a curtain and dumped dead along the same stretch of Interstate 580 that I drove every day. Yet, as disturbing as those scenes were, for some reason, it's the sounds I've heard, not the images I've seen, that linger the longest.

When I was ASAC Miami, our white-collar crime agents had partnered with the NTSB and FAA to investigate the cause of the 1997 crash of Fine Air Flight 101, a McDonnell Douglas DC-8 cargo plane that went down after takeoff from Miami International Airport on its way to the Dominican Republic. The plane was deliberately overloaded by twenty-seven hundred pounds. To compound matters, the load crew made the conscious decision to not bother locking down the cargo pallets, since they were already tightly and improperly jammed into the hold. Fine Air personnel criminally falsified their paperwork and then destroyed evidence after the crash. Decisions like these, without calculating or caring about the consequences, can have fatal results; this case was no exception. All four crew members on board, and a man on the ground, perished in a fireball.

The cockpit voice recorder captured the sounds of the captain and the first and second officers during their last minutes alive. First, I heard the pilots carry out their preflight checklist and receive permission to take off. All seemed normal until things quickly went south. I listened to the crew's confusion as to why their aircraft was rotating to vertical and wouldn't level off. In the background I could hear the thump, thump, thump of each unsecured, overweight cargo pallet slamming aft toward the tail and forcing the plane nose-up at an 85-degree angle. The stall warning alarms sounded in the cockpit as the pilots tried in vain to regain control. For a brief second it must have seemed like the big plane was suspended straight up in midair. But now, with the plane diving back toward the ground like a missile, desperate shouts and expletives filled the cockpit as the crew realized they were about to die. The recording ends with the sound of explosive impact. This was bad, but I've heard worse.

As a parent of young children, I found it particularly tough to supervise Crimes Against Children cases. And it was heartbreaking as a father myself to hear the long, anguished wails of another father as he tried mightily to tell a 911 operator what he was seeing in his own upstairs bathroom. John Lin had come home from work to discover his fourteen-year-old daughter slaughtered in a blood-soaked nightmare. Our San Francisco squad worked not only the plague of child porn but also a growing caseload of unsolved child abductions and murders. In fact, we had enough of those cold cases to theorize that we were dealing with at least one serial child predator in Northern California. In the quiet East Bay community of Castro Valley, Jenny Lin, a gifted young musician, came home from school like any other day; except this day, May 27, 1994, would be her last. Jenny's senseless killing remains unsolved, her brace-toothed smile remains in our minds, and her father's tormented 911 call remains forever in my memory.

Conservancy sometimes demands the ultimate sacrifice. The last thing you want as an FBI agent is to have a field office building named after you. That's because you'll never be there to see it. When an FBI agent pays that price, it might mean that their name gets permanently etched on the facade of their field office. The Newark FBI Field Division was renamed in honor of one of my own academy classmates, Barry Bush. Barry was fatally shot on April 5, 2007, in Readington Township, New Jersey, while working a series of armed bank robberies. Barry and his partners were in pursuit of four heavily armed bandits who had already fired their assault weapons inside two of the banks. Barry was survived by his wife, his mother, his son and daughter, and his brother and sister. If the FBI is a family, your academy classmates are like your brothers and sisters. We may scatter to the four winds after graduation, but a special bond always remains. Together we sweated and stumbled, punched and parried, wrestled and ran, and hollered encouragement at one another until we were hoarse. Even though it was years later, losing Barry caused all of class 87-16 to stop and reflect on the supreme sacrifice of a committed conservator.

Two of the field offices I helped lead were named after agents who gave their lives protecting our communities. One of the worst days in FBI history was April 11, 1986. That was the date of a gun battle in the Pinecrest area of Miami-Dade County between eight FBI agents and two serial bank and armored car robbers responsible for multiple murders over a seven-month spree. One hundred forty-five shots were fired in a withering gunfight around a chaotic convergence of cars after a deliberate collision with the suspect's vehicle. Agents Jerry Dove and Benjamin Grogan were killed, and five other agents wounded. The two suspects, William Russell Matix and Michael Lee Platt, were also killed. The agents were pinned down by a barrage of rifle fire, and even though Matix and Platt were wounded, they kept shooting. So did the agents.

Despite being shot multiple times, the agents kept engaging the gunmen, emptying their weapons, then grasping for backup weapons and ammo. Some of the agents had so much of their blood seep into the mechanisms of their guns that their weapons wouldn't work. As Platt slipped into Grogan and Dove's car and tried to start it, one agent, his arm already torn open by a round, and his partners lying gravely wounded around him, managed to march directly toward Platt and Matix and fire six rounds from his Magnum using only his good hand. That agent's fourth and fifth shots hit Matix in the face and stopped him. The agent moved to the driver's-side door, reached his revolver into the car, and fired his sixth and last round at Platt, finishing the fight. The heroism and bravery displayed on that day is the stuff of Bureau legend. If you ever visit the Special Agent Benjamin P. Grogan and Jerry L. Dove Federal Building in Miramar, Florida, spend a silent moment of respect at their memorial.

Miami wasn't my only field office to carry the name of an

agent who sacrificed his life. Other than being a street agent, the greatest job in the FBI is running your own office. I had the honor of leading the incredibly talented men and women of the Cleveland Division. Covering northern Ohio, FBI Cleveland had satellite offices in the "garden" spots of Akron, Canton, Elyria, Lima, Mansfield, Painesville, Sandusky, Toledo, and Youngstown. The Bureau's impressive main office building on Lakeside Avenue along the shores of Lake Erie bears the name of Johnnie L. Oliver, a special agent who was shot and killed in Cleveland in 1979. Oliver was chasing a fugitive, Melvin Guyon, wanted for kidnapping, rape, and armed robbery. Oliver and six other agents tracked Guyon to an apartment where they thought he might be. They were right.

When Oliver and another agent went through the front door shouting "FBI," Guyon, holding an infant as a shield, immediately shot and killed Oliver with one small caliber round through the heart. Guyon, just nineteen years old, crashed through a window in a hail of gunfire. Quickly placed on the FBI's Top Ten Most Wanted Fugitives list, Guyon was soon captured in Youngstown after yet another shootout with agents. Just eight years into his career, Oliver left a wife and three children behind. But Oliver's sacrifice soon became more to me than just the memorial plaque in our lobby and the name on our building.

Some thirty years after Oliver's sacrifice, his killer was once again up for parole on a life sentence. FBIHQ contacted me to discuss whether the Bureau should, as it had done in the past, take an official posture toward Guyon's parole. The director was willing to sign a letter to the parole board recommending against Guyon's release if that was the right thing to do. I asked our chief division counsel to locate the old file on the case and to get me contact information for Oliver's widow. As I pored over the well-worn case file, I studied the crime scene photos, which included Agent Oliver's lifeless body sprawled on the floor, his Bureau shotgun lying beside him, and the window Guyon dove from, and I read the test results on Guyon's .32-caliber revolver. There were news accounts of Agent Oliver's body being placed into an ambulance while disgraceful epithets, applause, and cheers rained down from locals who were all too happy to see a lawman carried out feetfirst.

The file detailed Guyon's feeble defense that he didn't know who the white guys in suits that came after him were, despite that the neighbors all conceded they heard repeated shouts of "FBI." More interesting, Guyon later made a claim that his cheap handgun had malfunctioned and accidentally fired a round into Agent Oliver's chest. Yet FBI laboratory testing was unable to make the gun fire off a round on its own. Besides, witnesses confirmed Guyon's statement to them that he admitted, "I shot the FBI." I reached out to Oliver's widow. She was troubled that Guyon was once again up for parole and supported and appreciated any Bureau effort to keep Guyon where he belonged. I drafted a letter opposing parole for Director Robert Mueller to sign, but I wasn't done yet. The parole board hearing was in a couple of weeks and the Bureau was permitted to send a representative. I asked my admin to book my travel from Cleveland to the United States Penitentiary (USP), Coleman, Florida, thirty-five miles south of Ocala.

USP Coleman is a high-security federal prison that houses drug cartel leaders, terrorists, and spies. At that time, Melvin Guyon wasn't the only Coleman inmate responsible for murdering an FBI agent. In fact, Leonard Peltier was serving two consecutive life sentences there for shooting and killing FBI agents Ronald Williams and Jack Coler in a 1975 shootout on the Pine Ridge Indian Reservation. I walked through the thick electronic doors of Coleman accompanied by a local FBI agent who knew his way around the place.

This was my first and only time testifying at a parole hearing. I figured there might be a large meeting room with a long table of parole board members and me sitting before them. I doubted Guyon would be there. I was wrong. The local agent and I, having given up our weapons, were led to a cramped, triangle-shaped, closet-sized room entirely dominated by a round table. We had to inhale deeply in order to squeeze into attached plastic seats jammed between the wall and the table. Next came one solo parole board member. She maneuvered against the opposite wall until she was able to slide into her chair at the table. Brief introductions and small talk were interrupted by a guard ushering Guyon into the room.

Guyon was a big dude. He stared down at the three of us before taking his seat on the open side of the table closest to the door. The guard stood outside the room with a line of sight through a glass window. The parole officer seemed visibly uncomfortable. I wasn't thrilled, either. The three of us were pinned in our chairs against walls while Guyon had freedom of movement. If Guyon got violent we'd be trapped seated at the table until the guard could get in and drag him off us.

Three decades after Agent Oliver's murder, Guyon had counted on the Bureau's not showing up. Maybe he thought that by now the FBI would just forget that he had murdered one of its own and let bygones be bygones. That wasn't going to happen on my watch. I had never met Agent Oliver, his wife, or his kids, but I was standing in for them now, speaking for their husband, their father. Even more so, I was speaking for the entire FBI, past, present, and future. There was nothing in Guyon's file indicating remorse. There was nothing indicating he had abandoned the ridiculous excuses that he didn't know who those feds were on that tragic day or the nonsense that his gun had accidentally discharged. In fact, Guyon had even had a recent infraction or two while at Coleman. They were small rule violations, but they were enough for me to point out that Guyon was not a model prisoner.

I went first. I started by presenting the signed letter from the director. I wanted to be clear that I wasn't here on my own; I was the director's representative in this room. Then I methodically described every detail of the day Guyon murdered Johnnie Oliver. I had charts and photos of the apartment layout. I had laboratory ballistic tests and trajectory lines. I had witness statements proving that Guyon knew the FBI was looking for him before the shooting, multiple descriptions of his escape, firsthand accounts confirming he knew that he shot Oliver, and concerning the subsequent shootout before he was finally apprehended. I placed graphic crime scene photos of Agent Oliver's body right on top of our table, smack in front of the parole board rep and Guyon. In our hot little room with no air circulation, Guyon began to sweat. Then he started to shake his head from side to side. He blurted out something like "I didn't know we were going to go over the whole case again, I thought this was a parole hearing." But I viewed my role as more than a speaker at a parole hearing. I was a conservator.

It was Guyon's turn after I had made my case that nothing in Guyon's file or prison record was enough to overcome the horror of the facts leading to his conviction in Illinois for aggravated kidnapping, rape, and armed robbery, nor his federal first-degree murder conviction for the killing of an FBI agent. Guyon took issue with the fact that I had been permitted to recount the evidence of his crimes. He portrayed himself as a model prisoner. When the board member asked him about his recent jailhouse infractions, Guyon chose to dispute them and their significance. In my closing comments, with Guyon glaring at me across the table, I seized on his continued portrayal of himself as a victim. Several weeks after the hearing, I got word that the parole board member had recommended denying Guyon's parole. For me, this wasn't about Guyon. It was about Johnnie Oliver and the thirty-six FBI agents killed as the direct result of an adversarial action.

That's the point of conservancy. It's about actively maintaining a cause, a principle, a mission, a value, or an entity greater than just you and your team. It's about fighting for something that's worth the effort. If my fellow FBI agents sacrificed their lives for our country, then I could certainly commit to preserving what they and our entire institution represented. And the beauty of a collective conservancy, where everyone is responsible for something bigger than themselves, is that it produces excellence. The excellence comes from the uniquely human capacity to see beyond self-preservation or herd survival and strive toward a common idea or value. Whether it's a team of bakery employees who view themselves as nourishing a community or a group of American citizens working to preserve democracy, we perform at our best when we're accountable for something beyond ourselves.

3

CLARITY

THE FBI HAS "BRIGHT LINES." THESE AREN'T JUST STAN-
dards, they are practically religious commandments.
Crossing a bright line gets you fired. Everyone in the agency
knows what the bright lines are because they are prominently
published and clearly enforced. The *Cambridge Dictionary*
defines clarity as "the quality of being clear and easy to understand." Clarity is a key component of the FBI's code. For example, no one can feign surprise if they are suspended without
pay or dismissed for drunk driving. There is nothing unclear
about it. But the Bureau's brightest line of all is "lack of candor
under oath."

My time in Bureau leadership taught me that individuals
who saw themselves as having particularly high integrity and
who possessed a generally inflated sense of self were more likely
to lie when confronted with wrongdoing than those who viewed

themselves as having just average integrity. These otherwise upstanding citizens, who were sometimes lay leaders in their church, former Eagle Scouts, and coaches of their kids' sports teams, simply could not reconcile the accusations against them with how they and others viewed them. They lacked clarity as to how their conduct conflicted with their cultivated image to the point of disbelief or denial. Senior executives are certainly not immune to this trap, as egos and self-images tend to inflate with rank. Even U.S. presidents are not immune to their own hubris. If my professional experience was illustrative, people lie not because the truth is inconsistent with who they are, but because it was inconsistent with who they think they are and want to be.

Interestingly, some of the most honest FBI employees I encountered in the disciplinary system were people I assessed as being smack in the center of the integrity spectrum. Although they violated the rules, they had enough moral integrity not only to understand they had done wrong but also to admit it and to submit to accountability. Their self-image and concern about perceptions didn't get in the way of owning up to what they had clearly done and clearly deserved.

An FBI employee who lies under oath is virtually worthless to the FBI, whether the lie is during an internal inquiry about candy bars missing from the break room or while on the witness stand in a criminal prosecution. There's federal case law behind this bright line, and the two most pertinent are known as *Giglio v. United States* and *United States v. Henthorn*. Agents and prosecutors refer to law enforcement officers who are proven to be dishonest as having "Giglio-Henthorn issues."

In the 1972 *Giglio* case, the Supreme Court decided that a prosecutor must tell the jury, and the defense, any information that tends to impeach the character or testimony of a prosecution witness. This included law enforcement officers. *Giglio*-related material included not only prior criminal records of witnesses but also other acts of misconduct by any prosecution witness. In the *Henthorn* case, the court held that with respect to potential impeachment information, the government is obligated, upon a defendant's request, to examine the personnel files of government employees it intends to call as witnesses in a criminal trial so it can determine if anything in the files ought to be made available to the defense. It's all about whether that particular agent can be trusted. For example, if an agent was found to have previously falsified a receipt on her travel expenses, that act of dishonesty might have to be disclosed if she ever testified in court.

The FBI goes even further than the case law. The Bureau requires each employee with a potentially impeachable issue in their file to disclose that issue to whatever prosecutor they are working with. FBI agents get transferred during their careers, which makes it difficult for field office and U.S. Attorney Office leadership to know which agents have which issues. During my days in the Bureau, even though prosecutors could and did pull agent's personnel files when required, the FBI took it to another level and required employees to disclose their baggage as soon as it looked like they could be called to testify. This "call your own fouls" approach to accountability is another element of *The FBI Way*.

The *Giglio* and *Henthorn* cases help seal the fate of any FBI agent determined to have not just shaded the truth, but to have lied while under oath. If that agent is a potential witness in a criminal proceeding, the prosecution would have to disclose the agent's file to the defense, the defense could impeach the agent witness as dishonest, the jury might be unable to trust anything the agent said or did, the prosecution could lose their case, and a bad guy could return to the streets. And agents aren't under oath just when they are in court. Agents are placed under oath even during internal administrative inquiries, which leads us to the case of the young agent in one of the Bureau's biggest field offices. He violated that clear bright line.

As described by the United States Court of Appeals, Federal Circuit (yes, the agent took this case all the way to the federal court of appeals): "While driving his official unmarked Bureau vehicle, the agent stopped another car he thought might be stolen." Beyond the fact that FBI agents don't just generally pull over stolen cars, there was also another problem. "The agent had an unauthorized passenger in his car: his daughter, whom he had just picked up at her day-care center on his way home from work because his wife (who usually picked up the girl) had told him she had a situation at work. The driver of the stopped vehicle became angry at the agent and reported the incident to the agent's supervisor."

Agents get government vehicles so they can do their jobs and respond to calls at any hour, not so they can pick up their kids at day care. Imagine if that agent was involved in a violent altercation or a high-speed chase with his daughter in the back seat. Unauthorized use of the bucar and having an unauthorized passenger in it can each merit a minimum thirty-day suspension without pay.

The agent's supervisor did the right thing and notified the field office chain of command. Covering up allegations or sweeping incidents under the rug are extremely rare in the Bureau. Two supervisory agents from OPR were assigned to investigate the citizen's allegation. They interviewed the agent. In the agent's signed, sworn statement he said, "This was not the only occasion I picked up my daughter with a Buvehicle. Similar emergency circumstance [sic] occurred once in December 1997, and once again in January 1998. Other than these three occasions, I have never had any other unauthorized person in a Buvehicle."

There was a problem with the agent's statement—it was contrary to the evidence. Specifically, day-care records as to who picked up the daughter, on which dates, were matched with electronic toll records marking the times the agent's bucar drove in the direction of the day care. The evidence reflected that the agent used his bucar at least fourteen times, and possibly many more, to pick up his daughter. My adjudication team studied the investigative report, including the improper pullover of the citizen, the unauthorized passenger, the time and attendance violations when we compared the times of day he picked up his daughter against the times he claimed to have signed out of the office, and the lack of candor under oath. We recommended the agent's dismissal.

This young agent became a cause célèbre in his office. His colleagues began an extensive letter-writing campaign the likes of which I would never see again. In my experience, character witnesses often knew very little of the facts of a case, in part because OPR didn't leak those facts, and in part because the employee was too embarrassed to share the whole story. The colleagues simply heard that a good guy they worked alongside might get fired. Nevertheless, this display of support was impressive. Letters arrived on my desk at headquarters stating that the agent was the finest, hardest-working, most respectful family man and combat veteran they had seen in a long time.

I analyzed the facts until they were committed to memory. I read and reread the agent's statement. I simply could not believe that an agent would end his early career by lying about the number of times he picked up his daughter in his bucar. The difference between three times and fourteen times was virtually inconsequential; if he had told the truth, he was looking at sixty to ninety days' suspension either way. I was concerned that the agent either might not have seen or might not have understood all the evidence that the investigators collected. I did not want to fire a respected agent, a military veteran, simply because he might be confused. Yet I also knew that if the evidence showed he was deceptive, the Bureau couldn't be saddled with him for the next twenty years. I decided to do something I had never done before as a unit chief. I called the head of the agent's field office, advised him that the agent was headed for dismissal, and said that I wanted the agent to travel to FBIHQ so I could hear directly from him.

At my request, the agent traveled to FBIHQ. At the appointed time he made his way to the secured doors of the OPR office space with spit shined shoes, a spiffy suit, and freshly shorn hair. We found a discreet room and sat down. I placed him under oath and told him point-blank that I had never invited an internal inquiry subject to speak directly with me, the adjudicator, because that was the job of the investigative unit. The FBI kept the internal investigative function separate from the adjudication function because they wanted a neutral and objective party deciding discipline, not someone who might have already made up their mind during a possibly long and contentious investigation. Avoiding even the appearance of impropriety is one of those critical elements of the FBI's code. Yet, I wanted to ensure absolute transparency and accuracy with this agent. I needed as much clarity about what this agent had done as the Bureau exercised when it made lack of candor under oath a fireable offense.

I explained the gravity of the situation and told the agent the facts of his case merited dismissal. I said something to the effect that it would be a shame to end a career over a lie about the number of times someone misused their government ride. I laid out every piece of evidence we had including the day-care records and the electronic toll records. In the agent's second signed, sworn statement he conceded that he deliberately excluded his knowledge of additional instances of bucar misuse in his first sworn statement, "for fear of causing me further problems." This was an admission that he lied. There was no choice but to recommend dismissal for his lack of candor. It was the clearest of the FBI's bright lines.

As a military veteran, the agent had an additional avenue for appeal open to most veterans employed by the federal government: the Merit Systems Protection Board (MSPB). The MSPB has a reputation for siding with veterans in disciplinary cases, and the administrative judge assigned to this case was no exception. I took the witness stand to explain the FBI's bright line against lack of candor. While I was still on the stand, the judge turned to me and said something like "Tell [FBI director] Louis Freeh his bright line is too strict." After the hearing, we learned the judge reversed the agent's termination.

At this point, the Bureau's lawyers understood this case was bigger than just this one matter; this ruling represented a challenge to the Bureau's standards. The FBI's Office of General Counsel appealed the ruling to the full board. The full MSPB reversed the administrative judge's initial decision but changed the penalty from dismissal to a 120-day suspension.

Instead of being relieved that he still had a job, the agent, having exhausted all his administrative options, took his case to federal court. But the FBI didn't back down when its standards were challenged.

On January 28, 2002, the U.S. Court of Appeals, Federal Circuit, found that "substantial evidence in the record supports the Bureau's determination that [the agent's] April 6 statement lacked candor." The court continued: "This is not a case of only a minor variation between what was stated and what the true facts were." "The gross disparity between the three instances he first admitted and the twelve to fourteen additional instances he admitted a month later indicates he must have known it was substantially more than three." "The Bureau may require the highest degree of candor from its agents." The court upheld a finding of lack of candor and affirmed the MSPB's 120-day suspension. More important, the federal appeals court decision affirmed the FBI's right to discipline employees who lie, regardless of what they were lying about.

Why was it important for me to share this story? You may be astounded that FBI lawyers defended, all the way to the U.S. Court of Appeals, a disciplinary decision about picking up a child at day care. But the case was much more than that. It was an attack on the Bureau's standards, the ability to enforce its code, and it illustrated how seriously the agency viewed the trust placed in it by the American public. Too often, when organizations have their most important standards challenged, they engage in a cost-benefit analysis to decide whether to defend their core values. Those organizations don't recognize that standards worth defining are standards worth defending. Maybe that's because those groups never really achieve clarity when they try to define their standards. Communicating what you most value is better done now than when all hell is breaking loose.

Clarity can be particularly elusive amid chaos. FBI agents are confronted with chaos all the time; it comes with the territory. On a good day, you avoid contributing to the pandemonium while it's going on all around you. On a great day, you can bring calm focus to the chaos and help make sense out of it. It's certainly possible, even desirable, to achieve clarity from within, but often there's some external force that slaps us in the face and causes us to focus. In fact, agents bring that kind of focus into people's lives all the time—sometimes at gunpoint.

THE NATION OF YAHWEH IS AN AFRICAN AMERICAN SPLINTER group of the Black Hebrew Israelites. The Yahweh movement began in Miami around 1979 with Hulon Mitchell Jr. as its founder. Mitchell taught that God and all the prophets in the Bible were black. This meant that black Americans were descended from the ancient Israelites. Mitchell went by the name Yahweh ben Yahweh (God, son of God) and demanded total loyalty to himself, since he was, of course, the son of God. The Nation of Yahweh had thousands of followers convinced that they could learn their true history from Mitchell. The movement also labeled Jews and whites as infidels and oppressors. Mitchell and his followers did enough good work in bad neighborhoods in different cities to earn respect in various communities. In fact, the mayor of Miami declared October 7, 1990, to be "Yahweh ben Yahweh Day." This was before the federal indictments. Before clarity could be achieved.

One reason the Yahwehs appeared to be cleaning up crime-plagued neighborhoods was because they were murdering people, including the homeless. In late 1990, Mitchell, along with sixteen others, were charged under the Racketeer Influenced and Corrupt Organizations (RICO) Act. The indictment detailed eighteen acts of racketeering, including fourteen murders, two attempted murders, arson, and extortion. The murders were heinous. There was a beheading, stabbings, shootings, and severing of body parts. There were arsons with Molotov cocktails tossed into victims' homes while they slept. Mitchell had ordered his "death angels" to wait outside the victims' homes with masks and machetes to prevent victims from escaping the flames. There were initiation rites where Mitchell told members to "kill me a white devil and bring me an ear." A federal appeals court judge wrote: "The instant case is arguably the most violent case ever tried in a federal court."

As the Miami grand jury inched closer to issuing indictments, multiple FBI offices began to plan for a series of simultaneous high-risk arrests. All Yahweh members pledged loyalty to their leader, and some had proven they would kill for him;

that's a tough crowd to arrest. Mitchell maintained a heavily fortified compound in Miami. The FBI's Hostage Rescue Team would fly in from Quantico and handle that site. But Mitchell also had a base in New Orleans and was known to stay there as well. I was in Atlanta, where we got word that the Yahwehs had just purchased an abandoned hotel on Lucky Street. Because of the pattern of violence and its link to a belief system, the Bureau worked the Yahwehs as domestic terrorism (DOMTERR). In Atlanta, DOMTERR was assigned to my squad.

In the days leading up to the takedown, we began discreet surveillance of the old hotel. No one was sure whether the Yahwehs were going to fix up the place and run it as a business or just turn it into another enclave. We needed to figure out how many sect members were in there, whether any of them were on the indictment list, and whether Mitchell himself might be in our fair city. We had strong intel that inside the old hotel was Mitchell's wife, Linda Gaines, who was known as Judith Israel (all of Mitchell's followers used the last name "Israel"). Linda, or "Judith," was on the indictment list. We knew that she, like most of the Yahwehs, would dress in an all-white robe when she was in public. We also knew she had bodyguards who drove her around in an all-white Lincoln Continental. We just lacked clarity as to where, in the name of Yahweh, Judith was.

Our surveillance team saw virtually no movement during the day, so we decided to run a night shift. That was the right call. Our squad partnered with the office's full-time surveillance agents to stretch already limited resources. Each night, a few young black males would pop out of the building and make a food run. They bought more food than they could consume, so they were likely feeding others inside. We'd see lights go on in certain rooms on multiple floors but had no way of confirming how many of those rooms were occupied. There was no sign of Judith, the white Lincoln, or the bodyguards. It was time to get creative. We enlisted the help of the local fire marshal's office. He agreed to have one of his inspectors try to contact someone in the building to talk about fire safety and a certificate of occupancy. One of our agents, dressed like a fire inspector, went in with him. That ruse allowed us to count at least half a dozen people inside, but if Judith was in there, we didn't see her.

A night surveillance shift, downtown in a major city, is always fascinating. You see all kinds of things when people don't know you're there, and Atlanta was no exception. But this surveillance got interesting when, one night, a couple of Yahwehs started walking the neighboring blocks as if they were looking for us. When they couldn't find us, they'd return to their building. This continued the next night when they became bolder. We were convinced they found a couple of our vehicles, and they made a point of walking right up to and past those cars. The following night, one of them had a camera. Sure enough, they found a surveillance unit and snapped a photo of the driver.

Our full-time surveillance agents operate undercover. They don't like it when a bad guy takes their photo. In fact, hypothetically, one of those agents just might decide to run up behind the guy with the camera, yank it out of his hands, and keep running. You know, hypothetically, it's something that could happen on a dark city street in the middle of the night. I'm just saying. To us, the Yahwehs' stepped-up surveillance detection was a clue that someone special had arrived. Maybe it was Judith. Perhaps we had missed her. Clarity was still evading us.

November 7, 1990, was takedown day. The grand jury had spoken. At 6:00 A.M., Miami, New Orleans, Atlanta, and other offices hit their targets. Wearing body armor and our blue-and-yellow raid jackets, we entered the lobby of what was becoming the Atlanta branch of the Nation of Yahweh. Two Yahweh members were on watch. One of them leaped up and reached toward a desk drawer but decided against it when he realized he was about to get shot. We announced that we had warrants and needed to see everyone in the building. We asked which rooms were occupied, and the two shaken sect members gave us the room numbers. About half a dozen groggy and bewildered followers were brought down to the lobby. Floor by floor our team climbed the stairs of the building, opened every door, and searched every room. There were no beds, just mattresses and sleeping bags and cots. This was a flophouse for a cult of killers. There was also no Judith. And no one was talking. But then we got a call.

Another field office had come up with an address for Judith during their own raids. It certainly wasn't our address. It was an uptown luxury condo building off Peachtree in Buckhead. Our supervisor pointed to my partner and me and told us to get going before someone tipped off Judith's guards. As we weaved through Atlanta's morning rush hour, we realized this made perfect sense. There was no way the son of God was going to allow his wife to sleep on the floor in an abandoned old hotel. Anyone this close to divinity had to stay uptown. We were closer to clarity.

We pulled into the driveway of the condo building and jumped out of the bucar. The main lobby door was locked. The garage door to underground parking was shut tight. We radioed the office, gave our address, and asked our radio operator to try and call condo management. Just then the garage door rolled open and a poor guy on his way to work did a double take at the sight of two armed FBI agents ready for battle.

We jumped back into our car, hit the gas, and positioned ourselves inside the garage before the door rolled back down. It was a tight fit and no one was going to get around us, especially not a Lincoln the size of a boat. Certainly not the white Lincoln screeching through the garage below.

We sprang from the bucar and stood directly in front of the gleaming sedan roaring full speed toward the two of us. In these narrow confines there was nowhere for anyone to go. My partner leveled his shotgun at the driver. I drew my .357 and aimed it at the bodyguard in the front passenger seat. I could see Judith in the back seat, dressed from head to toe in white. They were all dressed in white, and they weren't stopping. I was close enough to see Judith's mouth moving and saying something. Their car skidded to a stop with its grille inches from our legs. Sometimes clarity is a shared experience. We shouted commands for them to get out. We cuffed Judith and sat her in the back of our car. I asked her if she was Linda Gaines; she said her name was Judith Israel. Good enough for me. Clarity achieved.

Linda Gaines stood trial in Fort Lauderdale as the second-in-command of the Yahweh organization. At her sentencing, despite hearing evidence that Mitchell had sexually abused her daughter weekly from the time she was ten until she left the group at age fifteen, Gaines remained defiant. She was convicted of racketeering and sentenced to sixteen years in federal prison. Hulon Mitchell, aka Yahweh ben Yahweh, was convicted of conspiracy to commit murder and sentenced to eighteen years in prison. The FBI's takedown of the Yahwehs, and the convictions of their murderous members, brought a kind of clarity to their followers that cut through the convoluted, cockamamie creed of a brutal cult. It's often the FBI's role, through enforcement actions, to send a wake-up call that reminds entire communities of what's right and what's wrong. Yet it's far from ideal if we're relying on law enforcement for that kind of clarity. Ideally, engaged citizens, schools, organizations, churches, charities, media, and corporations all play a part in bringing clarity when conduct undermines our values.

ONE REASON THE BUREAU ACHIEVES RESULTS ON THE streets is because it maintains clarity in its own house. For example, almost every FBI employee can list the agency's investigative priorities in order. A clear understanding of priorities isn't just an exercise for bean counters. No matter what line of work you are in, carefully developed and understood priorities provide guidance and direction in times of confusion and grayness. Success, or the lack of it, in each priority was carefully measured in ways that mattered. I'm not talking about counting the number of arrests. I'm referring to measuring the true impact achieved in a community, a region, or across a national program. Defining and measuring what matters help achieve a kind of collective clarity across the Bureau. This same approach works for personal lives, sports teams, large corporations, and entire countries.

On September 11, 2001, the FBI, like the rest of America, was seeking clarity amid near total chaos. Just weeks before the attacks, I was back at Quantico for executive training. The course was designed for groups of field executives regardless of our investigative program responsibilities. About a dozen of us from around the country spent a week getting clarity on the latest practices, patterns, and policy changes that we needed to know to get our jobs done. These courses usually had an overriding theme based on whatever hot topic was trending. The refrain to this course, and to every management session around that time, was loud and clear: an attack was coming.

During this course, and others like it, high-level briefers from across the intelligence community shared with us a conclusion that we had already been hearing about in the field:

Something terrible was imminent. Whatever was about to happen would be very bad and very big. The intercepted "chatter" among known al-Qaeda leadership and associates captured excited and cryptic references to some type of large-scale terrorist attack in the works.

At a special dinner during our course, we were addressed by Cofer Black, then director of the CIA's Counterterrorist Center, and the future ambassador-at-large and coordinator for counterterrorism for President George W. Bush. Black was the architect of the CIA's strategy against Osama bin Laden and al-Qaeda. If dinner speakers are supposed to amuse and entertain, Black was a failure. Most of us sat stone-faced, our knives and forks abandoned atop half-eaten steaks.

When Black was done sharing his somber summary of the indicators pointing to an impending attack, our room full of type A gunslingers began to pepper him with questions:

Any chance you've got this wrong? (Not really)

Are we sure this will be an attack against the United States? (Yes)

Could it be an attack against U.S. interests outside our borders? (Probably not)

Do we think the operators are already here? (Could be)

Any idea of the nature of the attack? (Only that it will be large)

Why don't we know more? (The bad guys are speaking in code)

Why can't we grab them? (Not sure where they are; don't want to trigger attack)

We had plenty of concerns but zero clarity. The Bureau had already quietly begun an effort to stop what sounded like potential catastrophe. Agents started leaning on their sources, asking them to keep their ears open about a potential attack. Surveillance teams followed as many terrorism subjects as resources permitted. Court-ordered wiretaps that might typically be reviewed and translated after the fact were now covered in real time. We were desperate for an answer to the question on every intel officer's mind: What was about to happen?

The answer arrived on Tuesday morning, September 11, 2001, at 8:46 A.M. EDT. Ironically, I was in a crisis management lecture with other agents in a building next door to FBI Miami headquarters. I knew we were under attack as soon as I got the call that a commercial airliner had crashed into the World Trade Center. I stood up in the middle of the lecture room and asked all the agents to make their way back to their squad areas and wait for instructions. Every TV in our building was turned to the news. When I walked into my office, a group of employees was staring transfixed at the television screen. We watched as another plane hit a second tower. The entire office was silent.

I called my wife. She was at work and hadn't heard yet. She knew she might not see me for a while. She was right. It didn't take long for FBIHQ to send us the flight manifests from each of the four airliners. The Arab names of nineteen passengers jumped off the flight records. Fourteen of them were from Florida—our backyard. Fourteen. We opened our command center and activated our emergency response plan. Everyone was ordered back to the office. Each squad was assigned an investigative mission on either the day or night shift. The folks penciled in for night shift were told to go home and rest up, but they all refused to leave. The nation was being attacked. It was time for the FBI to bring clarity to chaos.

As we obtained addresses for each of our fourteen suspects, surveillance teams started monitoring each location. Were there additional suspects? Interview teams spread out across the area talking to neighbors, imams of local mosques, landlords, nearby business owners. Who were these murderers? How long had they lived amongt us? Once we obtained the hijacker's credit card records, every purchase had to be accounted for, each business questioned: Walmart, Home Depot, 7-Eleven.

The FBI's Evidence Response Teams (ERTs) faced a daunting assignment. FBI New York was dealing with the horror of the carnage at what was once the Twin Towers and what was now an unimaginable crime scene. All the debris would have to be sifted for human remains and to try and piece together each bit of plane, seat, or suitcase. Were there any identifiable belongings of the hijackers? Was there any evidence of explosives? One of New York's own agents perished as he attempted to rescue people in the towers. And a recently retired senior agent, on his first day on the job as head of security at the World Trade Center, died as he went back into the towers to save people. FBI Washington Field Office was responding with evidence teams to the destruction at the Pentagon. FBI Pittsburgh was leading evidence recovery at the site of the crater left by United flight 93 near Shanksville, Pennsylvania. And FBI Miami had an entirely different evidence task of its own.

Anywhere the fourteen South Florida–based hijackers had laid their heads had to be painstakingly searched for evidence. This wasn't just about taking photos, dusting for fingerprints, or grabbing trash or debris left behind. This entailed using virtually every technique in the FBI's evidence arsenal. Alternate light sources, DNA recovery, hair and fiber analysis, and more. And there was plenty of hair to analyze. When the first call came in from the ERT leader advising they had found a lot of hair, we were puzzled for a moment. Had we misheard him? It was soon determined the terrorists had shaved their body hair as part of a purification ritual prior to martyrdom.

As photos of each hijacker were publicized, our switchboard lit up with callers who had seen them or talked with them. Everyone had to be interviewed. And then came the hundreds of calls from area citizens worried that their brown-skinned neighbor was acting suspiciously and might be the next terrorist. All those concerns had to be logged, prioritized, and resolved. This scene was being repeated 24/7 across the FBI in every single office. In Miami, I led the night shift.

Like most impacted field offices, FBI Miami went to twelve-hour shifts for round-the-clock operations following 9/11. A command structure ensured there were supervisors and an executive manager on each shift. On paper, this allowed for proper rest and recovery during your "off" shift. But anything can look good on paper. I was the night-duty executive manager for weeks. After our shift had covered its assigned investigative leads into the hijackers, responded to thousands of tips from a concerned public, started to document our work, and briefed the next shift, we would head home for some daytime shut-eye. That's when our phones would start ringing.

So many leads poured in about the hijackers' daily lives and key interactions, concerns about possible accomplices, other terrorists, and suspicious individuals and packages that the complexity of any one lead often meant that it couldn't be resolved in one shift. Depending on how "hot" a lead was, the assigned agents would either keep working it beyond their shift or immediately hand it to the incoming team for continued work. The agents attempted to write up their notes before leaving the office. But they faced a choice between covering another priority lead versus immediately documenting the details of the last lead; we had to cover whatever was screaming in the in-box. To make matters worse, the Bureau's old automated major case system was struggling to keep up with the unprecedented deluge of investigative reports. That meant my bedside BlackBerry rang every time I'd begin to fall asleep. This went on for weeks. In a quest for clarity, sometimes you pay a price.

The calls came mostly from the staff reading our product in the 24/7 ops center at FBIHQ. Most calls would start with an apology, then launch into a question about whether a surveillance was or was not initiated, whether the ERT had or had not cleared a site, or whether someone's polygraph results had come in yet. This went on despite numerous field offices telling FBIHQ to stop waking people up. In one of the daily morning calls with HQ, the head of another field office had reached his limit. He blasted senior officials in Washington for turning key field managers into zombies. I was among those walking dead. The "off hours" calls slowed, if only for a while, as the field began to push FBIHQ toward some clarity of its own.

I like to think the FBI brought a measure of clarity to a reeling and confused nation after 9/11. In a remarkably rapid time frame, the Bureau and the U.S. intelligence community fully identified each of the hijackers, traced their origins, discovered who sponsored them, learned how and where they trained, and laid bare Osama bin Laden's role as the mastermind behind the attacks. I would never claim that the FBI's work after 9/11 was a success. No intelligence agency should claim success when the entire community failed in its primary mission to prevent the attack. Rather, the Bureau helped to restore order in the aftermath of one of the most tragic events in modern history.

SOMETIMES CLARITY CAN BE ELUSIVE EVEN FOR THE FBI. The Bureau is constantly dealing with matters that aren't what they appear to be. Agents know that it's dangerous to make assumptions, especially when lives depend on getting it right. The fog of a high-speed, high-stakes operation can cloud the sharpest minds and inject even more stress into an already tense scenario. That's why it's essential to interpret evidence without adding unnecessary assumptions. Medical students are taught "diagnostic parsimony," also known as "Occam's razor." That is, the simplest explanation is often the right one. Sometimes a headache is just a headache. And during the fall of 2009, in the middle of a wild cross-country race to disrupt a terrorist plot, a jihadi's encounter at an Ohio rest stop might just be, well, um, a "romantic interlude." Even for a Bureau surveillance team, clarity isn't always crystal clear.

After my stint in Miami, then two years as an FBI inspector and chief inspector, I was named the head of the Cleveland Division in late 2006. FBI Cleveland's surveillance team was always in high demand. They had been together for a long time, had become a tight unit, and got results. The Bureau's surveillance resources were coordinated by FBIHQ, who made the tough calls as to which surveillance team in which office would be deployed in support of which highest-priority cases. I might have wanted to use our team to tail a Cleveland drug network, but if Denver was running 24/7 shifts on multiple terrorists about to blow up the New York subway, Denver would win hands down. That's what happened in September 2009. Cleveland's surveillance supervisor stopped by my office to let me know that HQ had ordered our team out of town to support

Denver on some "really big case." At that point, the team was no longer working for me, but for SAC Denver and FBIHQ. I made a mental note that we would be without surveillance resources for the foreseeable future.

As I would learn only later, Denver was indeed working a major case. As was New York. So was any FBI surveillance team between Denver and New York. The case was code-named "High Rise." The investigation later became the subject of a book by outstanding *New York Times* reporters Adam Goldman and Matt Apuzzo: *Enemies Within: Inside the NYPD's Secret Spying Unit and bin Laden's Final Plot Against America*. In early September, emails were intercepted between the United States and a Yahoo account linked to an al-Qaeda operative in Pakistan who was part of a terrorism investigation. Someone in Aurora, Colorado, was seeking help with a recipe that included flour and a clarified butter used in Pakistani cooking. Whoever it was had been kind enough to provide his phone number in the email. When there was no response, the sender fired off another email just minutes later. That email got everyone's attention.

The second email read, "All of us r good and working fine, plez reply to what I asked u right away, the marriage is ready flour and oil." The word *marriage* was often used by al-Qaeda to refer to a planned attack. We theorized it had to do with their belief that martyrdom would bring a reward of seventy-two virgins in paradise. The FBI quickly discovered the Aurora email address and phone number belonged to twenty-four-year-old Afghan immigrant Najibullah Zazi. Mr. Zazi had lived in Queens, New York, and sold coffee from a pushcart near Wall Street. But a few months earlier he had moved to Colorado, where his aunt, his uncle, and more recently, his parents had relocated. At the time of his email, he was working as a shuttle driver to and from Denver International Airport, giving him insider access to the largest airport in North America. FBI intelligence analysts pulled Zazi's travel records and learned he had visited Peshawar, near the Pakistan-Afghan border. That was al-Qaeda territory. In fact, flight manifests and seat assignments showed that Zazi probably traveled there with two buddies—a taxi driver and a security guard, both from New York.

Zazi wasn't in Peshawar for a casual weekend holiday; he stayed for five months. Now he was back in the States and urgently emailing about "all of us" being "ready" for the "marriage," and talking about components of a recipe. FBI Denver put Zazi and his family under surveillance. They watched as Zazi's father took him to a Hertz rental car office and used his own credit card to get Zazi a car. Early the next morning Zazi slid into the driver's seat of a Chevy Impala and made his way to I-70. Wherever Zazi was headed, he was in a hurry to get there. Surveillance agents clocked him at ninety miles an hour and started to worry about losing him. They could either keep up with him or remain discreet, but they couldn't do both. Sometimes achieving clarity requires creativity.

FBI Denver decided to slow things down. At the Bureau's request, the Colorado State Patrol pulled Zazi over for speeding about an hour east of Denver. The trooper, now in direct contact with the FBI, was asked to try and find out where the hell Zazi was going. It worked. Zazi provided the trooper his rental papers. He also provided his destination—Queens, New York. Zazi talked about his coffee cart business, the Mets, and the New York Open tennis tournament. This was much more information than anyone offers on a routine traffic stop. The trooper sent Zazi on his way but noted that something wasn't right with this guy.

In New York, the Joint Terrorism Task Force (JTTF) was now working nonstop to gain clarity. Was Zazi part of a terror cell? Who were the members? What were they planning? When would it happen? And then there were the inevitable decisions the Bureau often faced. Should we disrupt this now and bring in Zazi and his crew for questioning? Do we have enough for an arrest warrant yet? Would a premature takedown cause other cell members to execute their plan? In Denver and New York, JTTF agents, analysts, and detectives were drafting affidavits seeking court-ordered wiretaps of the people communicating with Zazi. Denver worked to install court-authorized microphones in the residence and vehicles of Zazi's family and to obtain their internet and phone records. What agents began to hear and see was deeply troubling. All this while Zazi flew like a bat out of hell on an eighteen-hundred-mile sprint to New York. Along the way, a curious incident would happen that confounded us.

FBI surveillance units in state after state had been handing off Zazi like a toxic baton in a deadly relay race. Those agents figured they were following a possible terrorist but were never given the details. They just knew they couldn't lose him. They knew even more than I did about what their assignment was. The Cleveland team had taken over responsibility for Zazi in Indiana and was now trailing him at high speeds near Ohio's capital city.

Even terrorists need to take a leak. Just before dawn, Zazi pulled into a highway rest stop near Columbus. The agents positioned their undercover vehicles around the area, at varying distances from Zazi. One agent ensured that he had the "eyeball"—a line of sight on Zazi and his car. But this agent also kept his distance, not wanting Zazi to see the same vehicle twice during the trip. Zazi left his Impala, went into the men's room for a while, then came out to his car. That's when it got weird.

By this, I mean the Cleveland agent who had the eyeball thought he might have seen things in that dim morning light that didn't make sense. The agent thought that after Zazi got into his Impala, someone may have joined him in the front passenger seat. It was a male. This guy belonged to a white van parked near the Impala. The agent jotted down the van's license plate. But just minutes later, Zazi drove off alone, again at top speed. The Cleveland team hit the highway and hoped they wouldn't be stopped for speeding by a trooper. When they got into Pennsylvania, the Cleveland crew handed Zazi off to yet another team and turned back toward home. Their job appeared over, as the Impala barreled on to New York. Yet, as I would soon learn, Zazi had left behind a mystery for the Cleveland Division to solve. Here was that clarity thing again.

Cleveland's counterterrorism branch leader strode into my office to warn me that Mike Heimbach, the FBI's head of counterterrorism, was on the phone, wound up, and asking if I was around. Sure enough, Heimbach skipped the pleasantries when he was put through to my desk. My CT leader plopped himself down in my office to listen in. Heimbach was indeed torqued, dropping F-bombs. I told Mike I had no idea what he was talking about and suggested that he calm down. Mike's call was the first time I was told about operation High Rise or informed why Cleveland's surveillance team had been deployed outside the division. Until then we had operated under a need-to-know basis. This wasn't unusual because it typically didn't matter—until it did.

Our team's surveillance logs had just hit the Denver office. That's when an agent noticed something about a rest stop and a guy from a white van. I told Mike I'd get answers and come back to him. Our surveillance supervisor retrieved the logs and brought them to me. The report confirmed that one of our agents might have witnessed an odd encounter at a rest stop and that he was able to grab an Ohio license plate number. The supervisor also noticed that, surprisingly, no one had yet run that Ohio plate.

Even though the supervisor had just gotten chapter and verse from the surveillance agent, I needed to hear this for myself. I wanted clarity. We called the agent into the office. FBI surveillance teams are undercover, they don't drive vehicles traceable to the government, and they don't work in an office that says "FBI" on the door. So the agent had to be called and asked to make his way into the field office. He was a seasoned senior agent, certainly not a newbie to the surveillance squad. Dressed in street clothes, the agent settled into the wingback chair in my office.

He was tired. The whole surveillance team was exhausted from playing high-velocity leapfrog across America's highways in pursuit of a madman. They had never lost their target. The agent told me Zazi pulled into the rest stop in the twilight before sunrise. The small team scattered their cars around so someone could move out ahead of Zazi, while others could fall in behind him regardless of how, or how fast, Zazi left the area. The agent sitting in my office had parked his car on the edge of the rest area, many yards away, but with a line of sight to Zazi's Chevy. Once Zazi returned from the restroom, the agent saw another guy, walking behind our target, appear to get into Zazi's front passenger seat. For a few minutes, the agent lost sight of the new guy's head. It could have been window fog, or it could have been the bad lighting. A short time later, the guy was back in his van, and Zazi sped off on his journey to jihad.

Our agent hung back just long enough to get the van's license plate. Then the agent had to make a split-second decision. The rest of his team was already rocketing east on the highway, trying to keep up with Zazi while trying not to be seen. A teammate called out on the radio asking for the agent's "20." The white van was still parked. Instinctively, the agent, unsure of what he saw, peeled out of the rest stop to catch up and rejoin his team. Besides, he could always call in the van's license plate and have dispatch run it as soon as he caught a break. That is, if he ever caught a break and remembered to do it. But there was no stop in the action until the Cleveland team handed Zazi off to FBI New York's squad in Pennsylvania. The plate was never run.

As fast as the surveillance on Zazi unfolded, the investigation of him and his colleagues moved even faster. Evidence was found of bomb-making materials and chemicals, multiple cell members, and plans to target New York subways. Zazi conducted internet searches about hydrochloric acid. He prepared acetone peroxide for use as a detonator and held planning sessions in New York. Agents learned that a couple of months prior, Zazi and at least three partners had bought large amounts of chemicals from beauty supply stores in Colorado. The chemicals were known components of TATP—triacetone triperoxide—a favorite of terrorist bombers. Nine pages of handwritten instructions were found on how to make and transport TATP. Zazi was the real deal, and now, just maybe, someone had met with him in Ohio. Who was this mystery man? Were he and Zazi exchanging bomb-making material? Passing operational information or instructions? Clarity was in short order.

We ran the Ohio plate. It came back to a local Cleveland address in our own division. Of course. Not only that, but it belonged to a courier company located smack next to Cleveland-

Hopkins Airport. That meant whoever the driver was, he probably had unfettered access to loading areas at the airport. If Zazi had slipped the driver explosives, that bomb could now be anywhere. I called my executive management team into my office. We needed an agent to drive by the courier company and discreetly find that white van. We also needed the intelligence analysts to tell us everything about the courier company, its owners, and its employees. I asked for the entire JTTF to stop what they were doing and start working this white van mystery.

The Joint Terrorism Task Force concept is a beautiful thing. It is one-stop shopping under a single roof for virtually anything you may need from any local, county, state, or federal law enforcement or intelligence agency. Each agency dedicates at least one agent, cop, or detective full-time to work elbow to elbow with the FBI's counterterrorism squads. For example, in this white van caper, we needed to know the freight shipping history of the courier company. Had they shipped or received packages from the Middle East or South Asia, maybe Pakistan? Were there any chemical deliveries? The U.S. Customs agent on the task force quickly found those answers. Of course, the company had indeed shipped a variety of materials to and from Pakistan. Of course.

We were headed into the weekend. Ask any FBI agent on what day of the week emergencies are most likely to happen; they'll tell you it's always a Friday night. Our weekend was doomed as soon as the agent we sent to the courier company called us with an update. Although it was dark, the agent could see the company's parking lot was locked down, ringed by a security fence, and within the secure airport perimeter. The agent had one more detail to tell us. Although he couldn't get onto the property, he was close enough to report that the company had an entire fleet of white vans parked in rows behind the security fence. Well, of course it did.

I opened our 24/7 command center and activated the officewide response plan. That meant no one was leaving the office unless they were on the "midnight shift," in which case, those folks were to go home and sleep. While Denver was combing for more evidence of a terror attack, and New York was searching for bombs and bombers, Cleveland was now looking for the guy in the white van. We also couldn't rule out that this company could be the go-to courier for a terrorist network that might include jihadis in our own backyard. Since we didn't yet trust the management of the courier company or know if each driver used the same vehicle every day, I wanted surveillance on every white van coming out of that parking lot.

While that large-scale effort was getting under way, we needed to work through various theories about the rest stop. Were chemical precursors exchanged? Was money delivered to fund an attack? Was a coded message for Zazi mailed from Pakistan? By Saturday, we had developed a working theory on what might have happened. FBIHQ was expecting another update. We had an excellent Ohio state trooper assigned to our JTTF and asked her to dig into whatever her department knew about that rest area along I-70 in Columbus. The company was coming up clean, as were their international shipments tracked by customs. I called Mike Heimbach and told him we had a theory.

"Mike, the State Patrol tells us this rest stop is notorious for gay liaisons."

After a pause, Mike responded.

"Am I supposed to tell the director that this was all about a blow job?"

You might think it odd that a terrorist who perceived himself as fervently devout would violate his religion just prior to martyrdom. But not if you had investigated the 9/11 hijackers. Those guys, including ringleader Mohamed Atta himself, were reported by bar owners, strippers, and hookers to have caroused like it was their last day on earth. As far as we were concerned, anything was possible.

On Sunday, as hundreds of New York agents and officers suited up in tactical gear for multiple raids on members of Zazi's cell and on their storage sites, agents in Cleveland identified the van driver. He was white, young, with a clean record. That didn't mean he wasn't a terrorist, it's just that we couldn't find anything indicating he might be. Intelligence analysts in our office and at FBIHQ performed the high-tech equivalent of an autopsy, examining his online presence. There was nothing that raised any flags. Our surveillance team tailed him as he zipped around Ohio making deliveries. With coordinated raids about to occur in New York, we needed to move to the next phase of investigation.

The courier company had checked out clean just like the driver. I called the counterterrorism supervisors and case agents into my office and closed the door. I polled each of them as to whether it was time to approach the courier company manager, and ultimately the driver. Each one of them agreed the time had come. We couldn't tell the manager what was happening, so we concocted a story about the driver being a potential witness to a crime. It was a truthful cover.

One of our best counterterrorism agents headed out to approach the boss at the courier company. After what seemed like only a short time, that agent put us on alert: the manager advised that his driver wouldn't be available for a couple of days—because he was making a delivery to New York. About the same time, the team trailing the van reported that their target was driving east and traveling fast. Now we faced the possibility that our guy, maybe without even knowing it, had a bomb in a van streaking like a missile toward America's biggest city.

New York's simultaneous predawn raids had turned up nine brand-new backpacks stacked inside a green suitcase. That could mean one backpack for each of the suspected cell members identified so far. If these bags were intended to carry explosives into the subways, none of the suspects were admitting it. An electric scale and calculator were found in the closet of one apartment. And everyone had a different story about why they had traveled to Pakistan with Zazi. Evidence teams swabbed everything everywhere for traces of chemicals and explosives.

These high-profile search raids now meant that every suspect knew the feds were onto them.

NYPD and the JTTF decided to pull over the white Chevrolet cargo van, with its Ohio driver, now stuck in Monday morning traffic near the Lincoln Tunnel. They searched the van for bomb-making materials, jugs, bottles—anything used to store chemicals. They found nothing of the kind. The driver turned over his shipping papers and said he was delivering an eight-foot-long sign to the Macy's department store in Herald Square—the same place where the famous Thanksgiving Day parade terminates. Although that site would make an iconic target, the driver posed zero evidence of a threat. Police photographed the sign, the documents, and the van, and then sent the driver on his way. The search for clarity in the back of a cargo van turned up empty. Or did it?

Sometimes, when our pursuit of clarity about someone or something in our work or personal lives remains elusive, we need to ask ourselves whether we're confusing clarity with curiosity. By their nature, FBI agents want to know the root cause of everything. We have an innate desire to figure out why. That's a great trait to have unless the quest for clarity becomes a counterproductive and obsessive distraction from more important things we should be doing. In this case, I wasn't going to let that happen. The driver of the van didn't deserve to have his personal life exposed or questioned for the sake of curiosity. We had the clarity we needed. We closed our investigation.

Put simply, you need to know when it's time to stop. Sometimes we just need to accept that clarity might be either un-attainable or not worth the effort, especially when continued pursuit of the unknowable can take us off course. That Ohio van was still taking us off course.

We had all but concluded that the driver of the van had no terrorism connection. The only thing left for us to do was to sit down with him and ask about the mystery rest stop on I-70. The guy had a wife and kids, so we approached him discreetly. The agents who interviewed the driver displayed photos of Zazi and asked him about that brief pit stop near Columbus. He vaguely recalled making the stop but claimed no recall of Zazi or that rented Impala. Although the agents couldn't be certain, they found the driver believable. He took a polygraph and passed.

It was quite possible that our surveillance agent, who admittedly was uncertain of what he saw, had not seen anything. We could expend endless resources digging deeply into the driver's personal proclivities, but that would take us on a journey beyond our mission. I reminded myself that anything beyond some connection between the driver and the Zazi terror plot was more about curiosity than clarity. We had done our job. We had answered the terrorist threat question. I had sufficient clarity. It was time to move on.

Najibullah Zazi was arrested in September 2009 for being part of an al-Qaeda cell about to commit suicide bombings in the New York subway. The U.S. government alleged that the plot was directed by Saleh al-Somali, al-Qaeda's head of external operations, and Rashid Rauf, another al-Qaeda operative. Zazi pled guilty. Other cell members and associates were also convicted. Zazi's charges included conspiring to use weapons of mass destruction, conspiring to commit murder in a foreign country, and providing material support to a terrorist organization. Al-Somali and Rauf were later killed by U.S. drones.

The white van story was a reminder that we don't always need all the clarity we seek. And sometimes, even for investigators, we might have to accept that clarity will never come. For example, during my years in Atlanta, I was one of many agents assigned to the initial investigation of a series of mail bombs throughout the Southeast. The bombs killed federal judge Robert Smith Vance Sr., of Alabama, at his home, as well as black civil rights lawyer Robert E. Robinson, in his Savannah, Georgia, office. FBI behavioral scientists worked overtime trying to profile whoever it was that was sending the deadly packages. Their analysis was helpful in identifying the likely race, background, and age of the suspect and pointed us on a successful investigative path. But as is often the case when we seek to understand criminal motivation, our search for clarity can lead us into the trap of trying to apply logic to the loony.

Theories abounded as to why the mail bomber chose his specific targets, and what his specific beef was with each of those people and places. But when Walter Leroy Moody was finally apprehended and interviewed, it became clear that although his decisions made perfect sense to him, he was what we in the profession call "cuckoo for Cocoa Puffs." The FBI had found the "who" but was no closer to understanding the "why." Walter Moody was convicted in federal court and sentenced to multiple life terms. He was ultimately executed by lethal injection by the State of Alabama.

Almost thirty years after that mail bomb case, when I had become a national security analyst on cable news, I made a small discovery. One afternoon I was sitting on set at NBC headquarters in New York with a fellow contributor I've appeared with many times and deeply respect. My colleague's last name was Vance, and she was the former U.S. Attorney for the Northern District of Alabama. Might we have something in common beyond our TV network affiliation? In fact we did. Joyce White Vance lost her father-in-law, Judge Vance, to the tragic lunacy of Walter Moody. Realizing we had this case in common didn't provide any more clarity into Moody's mind, but it did remind me that sometimes we have to accept that for which there is no answer.

When we maintain clarity of purpose and principle, we remember what we stand for and who we are. That kind of clarity allows us to say yes to options when they reinforce our purpose, and even more important, to say no to choices we should just walk away from. Kind of like our curiosity about the driver of that white van.

You need to know when to demand clarity and when to just move on.

DURING MY STINT AS ASAC MIAMI, I WITNESSED A MEMORA-
ble example of the FBI declining a high-level request because it
would have undermined our effectiveness. This high-level request came directly to the SAC of FBI Miami from the attorney
general of the United States. Our response to the request would
serve as a lesson in clarity of purpose and mission.

On Thanksgiving Day, 1999, fishermen three miles off
the coast of Fort Lauderdale found a five-year-old Cuban boy
clinging to an inner tube. They rescued the boy and got him to
a hospital. His mother and eleven others on their raft weren't
so lucky. They drowned while trying to get to America. Little
Elián González was released from the hospital into the custody
of his uncle and other relatives in Miami. The next day the Cuban government delivered a note to the U.S. mission in Havana
demanding Elián's return. Two days later, Elián's father, di-
vorced and still back in Cuba, filed a complaint with the United
Nations demanding custody of his son. The U.S. State Department quickly recused itself from considering a child custody
issue and turned the question over to Florida courts. Eleven
days later, lawyers for Elián's Miami relatives countered with a
request that the boy be granted political asylum. International
media swooped into Miami to cover the drama of a small boy
trapped between his own father and freedom.

Elián and his family weren't the only players in this dramatic Latin narrative. The massive Cuban émigré community
in Miami despised Fidel Castro and what he had done to their

homeland. They saw Elián's plight as symbolic of all that was wrong with the Cuban government and all that they loved about America. On January 5, 2000, the Immigration and Naturalization Service (INS) announced Elián's father was responsible for his custody and Elián would be returned to Cuba in the next ten days. Thousands of Cubans from around south Florida took to the streets, most in support of keeping Elián in the USA, remembering that his mother perished trying to get him here. The tiny house where Elián was holed up with his relatives became the center of a three-ring circus composed of competing González family members, contrary state, federal, and foreign governments, and conflicted Cubans.

The lawyers were now in a high-stakes chess game as attorneys for Elián's U.S. relatives filed a state family court suit to have his uncle declared his guardian. Sure enough, a circuit court judge granted emergency custody to Elián's uncle. But U.S. attorney general Janet Reno wouldn't recognize the state family court's jurisdiction. Reno told Elián's local family that they had to file in federal court. She also lifted the January 14 deadline to return Elián to his father in Cuba.

Realizing the huge Cuban American voting bloc was in play, politicians and officials of all stripes started weighing in. Vice President Al Gore, the Democratic candidate for president, announced he supported legislation that would permit Elián to stay in Miami until the lawsuit was resolved in family court. Next, the U.S. State Department approved visas for Elián's father and close relatives to travel to America. And on

April 7, after meeting with Elián's father, Janet Reno declared that officials would be transferring Elián to his dad. But that was easier said than done.

AG Reno decided to speak with Elián's relatives in Miami to discuss how best to transition Elián into his father's custody. Over the course of the next several days, the relatives essentially told the attorney general of the United States to go pound sand. Dozens of armed Cuban American police officers from the City of Miami decided to set up a security perimeter around the home where Elián was staying. Those officers weren't just protecting Elián, they were sending a message that the feds weren't welcome there.

It was Good Friday and I was home having dinner with my family—until my BlackBerry went off. The SAC wanted his executive management team in the office. The boss wouldn't have called us in on Easter weekend unless it was a big deal. When I got to the office, I saw our SAC, the head of the Miami office of the Immigration and Naturalization Service (INS), the assistant chief of police for Miami, and a handful of INS agents I had never seen before. I also saw our FBI SWAT team leader. I quickly sized up what was happening, I just didn't know why it was staging at our place.

As the SAC explained it to me, he had received a call from FBIHQ telling him that it was time to get Elián out and that the FBI was going to do it alongside INS. Immigration did not have a traditional tactical capability, no SWAT team as we defined it, and precious little experience in high-risk entries and extractions. Besides, between the armed Miami police officers ringing the house, and the crowd of citizens outside it, an operation to safely remove Elián would need serious resources, the kind we had at FBI Miami. This kind of politically and socially charged operation could disastrously undermine the FBI's mission in Miami. That's why the SAC told HQ he wouldn't do it. He had clarity.

The FBI wears many hats in a community. Among its long list of duties, the Bureau trains police officers, educates kids about cyber dangers, dismantles gangs, infiltrates drug networks, arrests corrupt officials, identifies terrorist cells, and catches spies. None of that gets done without community liaison, trust, respect, and, in criminal and national security cases, cooperators who decide to work for the good guys. There are over one million Cubans in the greater Miami area. If someone in an FBI raid jacket ripped Elián from the arms of his loved ones to return him to the Castro regime, that's potentially one million citizens who would slam the door on the next FBI agent they encountered. The SAC spoke directly with AG Reno.

The attorney general was a friend of FBI Miami. Whenever she could escape the confines of Washington, Reno was back home in our neck of the woods living in the same rustic house that her mother built near the Everglades. The FBI provides security for only two officials; one is the director and the other is the attorney general. A Washington, D.C.–based protective detail covered the AG when she was in the nation's capital and traveling on business. But when she was home in Florida on weekends and holidays, she was primarily ours. The agents loved working with the down-to-earth, kind, and calm lady from the Everglades. She loved them back.

The SAC and the AG struck a compromise. The FBI would provide INS logistical and communications support, tactical guidance, and a place to stage and brief their team. FBI Miami would also be ready for the worst—a possible failed mission where an injured or trapped INS team had to be rescued by FBI SWAT. On top of that, there was planning to be done for protection of our own office and federal buildings in the event the whole city started rioting once Elián was in custody. The AG agreed.

AG Reno and Deputy AG Eric Holder kept White House chief of staff John Podesta briefed. Podesta updated President Bill Clinton throughout the night. It was going to be an all-nighter, but ultimately the INS executed its mission. They got Elián out of the house, but it wasn't pretty. Around the world, photos were published of INS agents wrestling a frightened young boy out of his family's arms. The FBI had escaped the turmoil that was just beginning. Clarity on who you are, and what your mission is, can be just as important as understanding who you are not, and what you should never do.

In fact, the assistant chief of Miami PD, a friend of the Bureau, had a very clear understanding of what his Cuban American officers would and would not do. That night in our command post, he told us with confidence that those police officers surrounding Elián's safe house would not step aside for INS agents. As a solution, he offered himself up as a sacrifice. He matter-of-factly stated that the only way this would work was if he was in full uniform in the front seat of the INS vehicle and for him to personally motion the officers away.

To understand how ballsy a move this was, you need to understand Miami.

The assistant chief knew this would end his career. The mayor, Joe Carollo, was Cuban American and had sided with Elián's Miami relatives. Carollo and other mayors in Dade County had defied federal authorities by announcing that their departments would not assist federal agents if they tried to take Elián from his relatives and return him to Cuba. Miami's assistant chief told his own boss what was about to happen, and wisely, that chief did not tip off the mayor. Following the INS raid, pandemonium broke out among thousands of protesters on Calle Ocho in Little Havana, and three hundred protesters were arrested. Within twenty-four hours, Mayor Carollo demanded the city manager terminate the chief of police for not giving him advance notice of the raid. The city manager refused, and Mayor Carollo fired the manager at a jam-packed city commission meeting.

At a news conference the next morning, the city's police chief, a twenty-five-year veteran, said he could no longer work for Carollo. The assistant chief, himself a twenty-five-year career cop, resigned. The assistant chief may not have been an

FBI agent, but on that Easter weekend, he embodied the Bureau's motto of Fidelity, Bravery, Integrity. Those two law enforcement professionals knew their loyalty was to the rule of law, not to a politician. I'd say those two leaders had clarity of purpose.

Clarity serves three purposes in our lives. First, it helps us stay focused on what matters most to ourselves, our families, and our organizations. Second, it drives people and teams toward successful resolution of common goals and objectives. Last, clarity teaches us when to move on.

4

CONSEQUENCES

THE ELEMENT OF SURPRISE WORKS GREAT IN A SWAT raid. But it's a terrible approach to doling out discipline. Even a parent with unruly kids in the back of the minivan will issue a warning about what might happen next: "Don't make me pull this car over." Arbitrary and random disciplinary decisions undermine adherence to standards, erode credibility, and violate fundamental fairness. An approach of "He didn't know what hit him" might correct conduct in the moment, but it won't win hearts and minds to achieve lasting results. It's essential to establish and communicate the likely consequences of misconduct whether you're developing a corporate compliance program, addressing behavior in a school setting, or preserving the integrity of the FBI. In the Bureau, the Office of Professional Responsibility (OPR) maintains "disciplinary ranges" for specific offense codes and makes those anticipated consequences accessible to employees. This practice helps keep both decision makers and employees on the same sheet of music, or at least in the same hymnal.

We all know that consequences are the results of our actions, but few of us want to face those repercussions when they're negative. Yet a code without consequences is mere window dressing, and at worst, a dangerous con game. It's dangerous because a code that's not enforced quickly becomes a lie that undermines your entire operation. You can't just wish a code into compliance; people need to understand that there's a price to pay if they endanger the collective health of the larger team. Consequences put the teeth in a code. And everyone has a role in the care and maintenance of those teeth. If you leave your dental care entirely up to your dentist and skip your daily flossing and brushing, you're going to have problems. The same goes for leaders and team members who think consequences are inconvenient, unpleasant, or someone else's job. Their code, and ultimately their group, is destined for decay.

Codes of conduct, particularly in the corporate world, are often deliberately vague. They don't articulate specific consequences for rule breaking. Corporate types say they like the freedom to decide whatever penalty seems appropriate for a given scenario and that they can't possibly foresee every act of misconduct. Yet disciplinary categories need not be precise or all-encompassing. The Bureau's range of discipline for specified offenses is often quite broad. For instance, the disciplinary range for drinking and driving begin at a 30-day suspension but could result in dismissal depending on the severity of the incident.

On November 23, 1999, a Miami Division agent, still within his two-year, new agent probationary period, polished off most of a pitcher of beer while watching *Monday Night Football* at the Quarterdeck Seafood Bar and Neighborhood Grill in Davie, Florida. He then headed to his home in Coconut Creek. It was about 2:00 A.M. when the phone next to my bed rang. Middle-of-the-night calls were not unusual for an FBI ASAC, especially in Miami. Tactical operations could develop quickly, kidnappings could unfold, but nothing good happened at 2:00 A.M. After I'd been in this management role just several months, my wife had developed a semiconscious response to the sound of late-night phone rings that involved scooping up her pillow and plodding upstairs to the guest bedroom.

The voice on the other end of the phone was the coordinator of the Employee Assistance Program (EAP) for FBI Miami. She explained that the SAC wanted her and me to go to an agent's residence, advise his live-in girlfriend that he had been in a car accident, and take her to North Broward Medical Center, where the SAC would meet us. When I asked the EAP coordinator about the condition of the agent, she told me that he would probably be okay, but that there were fatalities in another car. I was awake now.

Soon after the agent left the Quarterdeck and drove onto I-95, his car collided with the vehicle of Maurice Williams, twenty-three, a youth minister, and his half brother, Craig

Chambers, nineteen, a college student. The two were reportedly returning from choir practice. The agent was white; the two deceased half siblings were black. Williams worked with young people and dreamed of pastoring his own church. Chambers was studying to be a computer engineer. Florida Highway Patrol (FHP) investigators initially concluded the brothers were driving in the wrong direction on the highway, but one month later, in the face of mounting questions and community outrage, the FHP apologized and reversed their findings. Neither Williams nor Chambers had drugs or alcohol in their systems. Two sets of tests found the agent's blood alcohol content (BAC) to be nearly twice the legal limit.

The agent was charged with manslaughter and vehicular homicide, but after a trial of twenty days and deliberations over the course of two and a half days, the jury could not conclude whether it was the agent or the brothers who caused the accident. Instead, three years after the fatal crash, the jury found the agent guilty of misdemeanor charges of drunken and reckless driving. The agent was sentenced to ninety days in jail. The area's black community staged traffic slowdowns in protest of the acquittal and what they viewed as a lenient sentence.

While the court system took three years to arrive at a conviction, the FBI took less than five months to comprehensively investigate and adjudicate the agent's fate. The SAC called me into his office when the agent's termination letter arrived in the mail from FBIHQ. I thought maybe he might ask me to handle the unpleasant task of delivering the letter to the agent at home, but I should have known from past terminations that that wasn't his style. "We'll both go," he said. "The worst news has to come from the top." It was part of *The FBI Way*.

You see, by the Bureau's tough standards, it didn't matter whether the agent had or had not gone in the wrong direction on I-95 or if he caused the fatal accident. The agent went "the wrong way" when he violated FBI regulations by drinking himself into a daze and getting behind the wheel of a car. The death of two young men served as aggravating circumstances and turned what might have been a thirty-day suspension into a dismissal. The fact that the agent was still considered probationary at the time of the incident allowed the Bureau to move more swiftly and in a way that cushioned the blow to the Bureau's public perception. We could never bring back Williams and Chambers, but we could begin to restore the public's trust in the Bureau.

EXPERIENCED AGENTS AND FBI LEADERS BECOME ADEPT AT calculating the potential consequences of each tactical and strategic choice available to them. From a street-level undercover drug buy all the way to the geopolitical fallout when a foreign diplomat is nabbed for spying and booted out of our country, we learn to rapidly process the options and the impact in the form of decision trees that portray "if this, then that." While this kind of "seeing around corners" may be common in all manner of industry, the Bureau version is distinguished by an overarching adherence to doing what's right even when the consequences will hurt. In contrast, some companies or leaders avoid actions when the results will be personally or professionally painful. A pharmaceutical company that continues to sell its pain drug, despite knowing that it's highly addictive, is deciding to avoid the consequences of lost revenue by choosing profit over integrity. FBI leaders often make decisions despite the consequences, not instead of the consequences. Bear with me as I share a particularly gut-wrenching example.

A disturbing audio recording triggered the Bureau's decision to deliberately compromise a classified terrorism investigation in favor of an even higher purpose. On November 6, 1989, the Palestinian parents of a sixteen-year-old girl stabbed their daughter to death in the kitchen of their St. Louis apartment. This was a Muslim "honor killing" stemming from the daughter dating a non-Muslim boyfriend and having the audacity to get a part-time job outside the home. What the parents didn't know was that the FBI had lawfully obtained electronic surveillance authority for their home as part of a terrorism investigation. The haunting screams of the daughter and the unthinkable utterances of her father and mother were captured by an FBI microphone.

Ironically, the FBI terrorism case did not involve concerns of an imminent attack, so the resulting recordings were not "live monitored" but were instead reviewed after the fact. This recording, revealing the sounds of a mother and father murdering their own daughter, was the worst I have ever heard. It was played for us in specialized counterterrorism training. The purpose of making us listen to it was not only to expose us to the belief system around honor killings, but to teach us a lesson in organizational ethics. The instructor asked us, a class of street agents from around the field, how we would handle the discovery of a murder, which was not a federal violation, on a classified counterterrorism recording that, if revealed, would blow the Bureau's secret case on an entire Hamas cell. The class feebly lobbed options at the instructor, but we knew there was only one right answer: declassify the recording, hand it to the local police, and blow our case.

It's important to understand that this real-life scenario would not be handled the same way in other countries, or perhaps even by other agencies. Arguably, there were alternatives to blowing the Hamas case, especially if an agency operated by a different code than the FBI. An anonymous tip could be provided to the police. Or the tape could be used to threaten the parents with prison and "flip" them into informing on Hamas. In an amoral culture, one with no concept of the rule of law, a secret security agency might even send the recording to Hamas leadership, who might view the murderous parents as a liability and have them killed so they wouldn't expose their cell. Heck, maybe the whole cell would be killed or extracted; wouldn't that solve everything?

These weren't options for an agency expected to uphold our laws and defend the U.S. Constitution. The higher-level consequences to the Bureau's collective conscience would be far worse than losing one terror investigation if the recording was not declassified and handed to the police. There would be other means of neutralizing the Hamas cell, but there was only one way to bring justice to homicidal parents. You may never deal with a moral quandary over solving a murder or dismantling a terror cell, but you most certainly will encounter a choice between doing what's right and doing what's easy. You'll be tempted to justify the easier choice by convincing yourself that the end justifies the means. You'll regret that. The Bureau declassified the recording and provided it to the police. In 1991, Zein Isa and his wife, Maria, were convicted in the stabbing death of their daughter, Tina. Ultimately, the consequences caught up with their unforgivable crime.

SOMETIMES WORK, POLITICS, PEOPLE, AND LIFE IN GENERAL reveal gaps in code and consequences that cause us to think, *That just ain't right. Someone ought to do something about that.* Most likely, that someone should be us. During my Bureau career, there were times when it was clear that existing law hadn't caught up with the harsh reality of a crime trend we were seeing in the field. In fact, back in the 1990s, when it came to economic espionage and the theft of trade secrets, there were really no laws at all. Increasingly, counterintelligence cases in places like the Silicon Valley computer industry had turned from traditional cloak-and-dagger spying to outright theft. But trying to find a law that adequately addressed the loss of a formula or research line worth millions of dollars in future market value was like trying to use a shoplifting charge in the art heist of a Rembrandt. The consequences didn't fit the crime.

One of our cases in Palo Alto, California, served to highlight just how much the high-tech industry had become a modern-day version of Wild West lawlessness. Guillermo "Bill" Gaede was an engineer and programmer, first at Advanced Micro Devices (AMD) in Santa Clara, and then at an Intel Corporation facility in Arizona. While working at AMD, Gaede covertly gave technical semiconductor secrets to the Cuban government. He then left AMD and got hired by Intel, the maker of the prolific Pentium chip. That tiny microprocessor powered virtually everyone's desktop computer, to the point that its name became synonymous with the term "PC." The Pentium was Intel Corporation's crown jewel, and now Gaede worked within the jewelry store. This heist was going to be an inside job.

Gaede used a decidedly low-tech method to steal a quintessentially high-tech secret. Working remotely from home and using a computer terminal provided by Intel, he propped up a big clunky video camera and recorded the grainy images on his screen while scrolling through the designs for manufacturing the Pentium chip. Gaede then hightailed it to South America with one of the most valuable secrets in the computer industry contained on a store-bought videocassette worth about two bucks. According to later public statements by Gaede, he sold his employer's processor blueprints to representatives of China and Iran during that trip to Latin America. When we learned

Gaede was headed back home to Mesa, Arizona, we gave FBI Phoenix a heads-up and hopped on the next flight from San Jose. We were going to arrest a spy. All we needed was a law to charge him with.

In 1995, the federal criminal code hadn't caught up with the increasingly common reality of trade secret theft. After consulting with the U.S. Attorney's Office in the heart of Silicon Valley, the best law we could come up with was the Interstate Transportation of Stolen Property Act. That was a very old statute drafted to address what was then the burgeoning problem of car thieves crossing state lines with stolen automobiles. The statute required that the proceeds of the theft be valued at $5,000 or more. Intel executives were certainly prepared to say that the lifeblood of their company was worth more than five grand, but there was no legal precedent for how to demonstrate the value of intellectual property in a criminal case. Even worse, the very concept of intellectual property was untested in federal criminal court. For all we knew, the entire Pentium process might come down to the price of the two-dollar video cartridge Gaede recorded it on. In this case, using this statute, there was a very real chance that the consequences were not going to match the severity of the crime.

On a Saturday morning in September, the two case agents and I touched down in Phoenix and headed for the home of the federal magistrate on duty that weekend for the district of Arizona. We quietly sat in his small living room while he carefully read our charging document detailing the theft of secrets from two of America's biggest high-tech firms by a foreign-born mercenary spy. He reviewed the old stolen car statute. He gazed around the room at no one in particular, his head tilting from side to side like a puppy pondering something strange and new. He read the entire document again. Then he signed the warrant for Gaede's arrest.

We soon had Gaede in handcuffs. Our culprit would eventually be convicted and sentenced to thirty-three months in federal prison. It was a slap on the wrist for the potential damage done to America's dominance in the computer industry. Two extremely talented FBI case agents and a tenacious federal prosecutor worked their tails off to make this case. The disappointing consequences levied upon Gaede left everyone who toiled on the investigation feeling a bit like the country singer Deana Carter in her song from around that time entitled, "Did I Shave My Legs for This?" Yet our case had caught the attention of FBIHQ. I got a call from Director Louis Freeh's office. Freeh had taken a personal interest in the lack of legislation to adequately address trade secret theft, particularly when a foreign power was involved. Freeh understood that consequences could never match a crime that didn't even have a name. It was time do something about that.

The FBI wasn't allowed to directly lobby for specific legislation. But that didn't mean we couldn't gather the right people together and stick them in a room with lawmakers. So FBIHQ tasked me with visiting one-on-one with the top Silicon Valley CEOs and convincing them to testify on Capitol Hill. It was a tall order. It meant asking powerful corporate leaders to pub-licly acknowledge that their companies fell into one of two categories—those who were already victims, and those who were victims but didn't know it yet. That kind of admission could impact their stock price, incur the wrath of shareowners, and cause board directors to demand answers. Sometimes do-ing the right thing brings unpleasant consequences. HQ told me that if I could pull off this assignment, they would ensure a hearing took place on the Hill. I had my marching orders.

My first visit wasn't to a CEO. I knew that if I was going to convince these powerful icons to take a risk and expose their corporate underbellies, I had to make it less risky. They needed to feel comfortable that if they traveled all the way to D.C., tes-tified as victims of economic espionage, and put their brand reputation on the line, something good was likely to happen. No leader wants to be labeled a loser by his board or his share-owners. I had to get their comfort level up about the odds of a meaningful new law being passed to address the theft of trade secrets. I dropped by the office of congressperson Zoe Lofgren, who represented the district considered to be the heart of Sili-con Valley. Not only did she totally understand the gap in the law, but she pledged to draft and champion new legislation to protect the livelihoods of her many constituents employed in the high-tech industry.

Lofgren's support proved critical as I made the rounds to visit some of the biggest names in Silicon Valley. My strategy was to get the most respected CEOs on board first. I ditched my usual suit and tie to better fit in among the jeans-and-sneakers techie culture and to not draw attention to myself. My fashion ploy didn't work. With each scheduled appointment, some CEO's executive assistant would spot me in a crowded reception lobby and remark, "You must be the fed." So much for discretion. Even so, each of my meetings eventually ended in success. This wasn't easy; the CEOs had all the valid and predictable concerns. Yet once they heard that their peers had agreed to testify and that their congressional representative had their backs, they decided to head for D.C.

The Economic Espionage Act was passed in 1996. The new law allowed the federal government to meaningfully prosecute the intentional theft, copying, or receipt of trade secrets by individuals, organizations, or companies. And finally, the consequences matched the crime. Conviction included the possibility of imprisonment for up to ten years, with fines of half a million dollars against individual defendants. If a corporation was found guilty of such theft, the fines would rise to $5 million or three times the value of the stolen trade secret, whichever was greater. Importantly, if a foreign government was behind the theft, prison time jumped to fifteen years and fines could be doubled. It was all part of the FBI's commitment to fair and just consequences whether dealing with federal law, civil liberties, or even human life.

We should all commit to ensuring fair and just consequences in our personal lives and across our communities. It might mean adjusting our code to cover some new conduct that needs to be addressed or crafting consequences where none previously existed. If we're going to successfully do that, we have to maintain a kind of vigilance over our values, as individuals, as organizations, and as a nation.

IN THE BUREAU, WE WERE CONSTANTLY WEIGHING CONSE-quences, and engaging in second- and third-order thinking that required us to make quick, often life-and-death calls, based on available data. Should the SWAT team hit the house full of hostages now or wait until we were certain of the exact location of everyone in the house? How many hours has this tactical team been lying motionless in the rain and how long is too long to expect them to operate at full capacity? Some-times, often regularly after 9/11, senior FBIHQ executives had to weigh in, as part of the intelligence community, on whether today was the day that a known enemy combatant overseas would meet Allah. The consequence of those decisions liter-ally ended lives.

You may think it's a bit extreme to use a terrorist's neu-tralization as an example of a consequence for undesirable conduct. But it's merely a reminder that we need clear, com-mensurate, and enforced responses to that which threatens our code. A family, a company, or a country that's shy about trig-gering established consequences can expect boundaries to be repeatedly pushed to the point of breaking. Once that happens, your group's well-being is jeopardized.

5

COMPASSION

I MADE TOUGH CALLS IN HUNDREDS OF INTERNAL DISCI-plinary cases during my tenure as an OPR unit chief. I touched even hundreds more when I entered executive management and led field office and headquarters teams. I still remember most of those cases and the role that compassion played in the process. But perhaps the case that left the deepest mark involved the agent who drove his wife and kids into the city, to score his spouse some heroin. Yes, you read that correctly. An FBI agent drove his wife and children from the suburbs into the inner city to find heroin. Automatic dismissal from the Bureau, right? Not necessarily.

My favorite definition of compassion is "the sympathetic consciousness of others' distress together with a desire to alleviate it." The inquiry into this Bureau family's distress called out for compassion. Our internal investigative report on this agent outlined a waking nightmare. His wife had mightily struggled with a heroin addiction that few people, if any, knew about. Concerned about the potential impact on his reputation and career, and due to personal embarrassment, the agent was reticent to reach out for available assistance from the Bureau. Instead, the agent juggled getting his wife to professional help, arranging daily care for their young children, and working incredibly long hours on priority cases. The balancing act collapsed when the agent was unexpectedly called in to support a major case on a day when his arranged childcare had canceled. His wife was violently ill, experiencing all the symptoms of withdrawal from their latest attempt to end her addiction. There was no way she could care for herself, let alone their children. His in-laws and neighbors were unavailable. The agent was frantic for a solution to avoid letting down his family and his work team. He had reached his breaking point.

He piled his sick spouse and confused kids into the car and drove to the city to find the fix his wife needed to get through the day. With some guidance from his wife, the agent eventually found her a willing seller. They made the purchase and returned home. It was a devil's bargain. His wife would be cloudy, but conscious enough to keep one eye on the children until the agent could make it back home that night.

Unbeknownst to the agent, a law enforcement informant was involved in the agent's drug transaction and reported it. The Bureau's OPR investigators tore into the agent's story and came back with a tale of horrific judgment under severe stress.

After the file had made its way into our adjudication unit, one of our best team members poked his head into my office to tell me what he had. "Hey, boss, just a heads-up. We've got an agent who drove his wife to buy heroin." I replied with something like "And we're firing him, right?"

Yet we didn't fire him. It certainly helped that the troubled husband and father had been truthful during the entire inquiry. We got his family and him help through the FBI's exceptional Employee Assistance Program. Don't be mistaken. The agent got slammed with a sizable suspension without pay, but the cavalry was sent in to help. Treating one another like family was *The FBI Way.*

In the FBI, compassion is an essential component of consequences. Compassion provides the necessary balance to what could be an otherwise harsh and cold process. As sure as people need to know that their leaders have set bright lines on conduct, they also need to trust that those leaders will treat them as valued human beings. That's why good leaders take a holistic approach to weighing consequences by assessing an employee's total record, the context that led to their lapse, and that team member's capacity to overcome their wrongdoing.

Compassion also means recognizing when an employee's conduct might be a symptom of the dysfunctional system in which they work. The Bureau wouldn't hesitate to respond to identified patterns of conduct that might mean a problem existed with how the organization was doing business. During my later stint as the FBI's chief inspector, our teams investigated all agent-involved shootings. As quickly as negative trends were discovered, advisories or remedial training would be developed and disseminated to the field. If FBI SWAT teams were increasingly firing their weapons during high-risk car stops because cornered felons managed to crash their way through our vehicles, retraining was ordered on locking bumpers during a car stop.

While in OPR, I encountered a couple of cases involving undercover agents who were caught committing petty crimes, like shoplifting. Psychological studies of undercover personnel across law enforcement identified a kind of "undercover syndrome" with a host of physical and mental maladies linked to the stress of undercover work. As I came to understand, one of the identified responses to sustained undercover assignments was the "need to get caught" in order to reconcile the guilt associated with a very good person who had to regularly pretend to be very bad. Further, there was sometimes a "loss of self" that occurred in long-term undercover assignments where the agent lost the ability to turn the role-playing on and off. The Bureau studied each such instance and implemented strong programs that monitored and supported undercover agents, improved their selection process, and mitigated risk.

Compassion infuses fairness into a system that could easily become unforgiving. Just outcomes are more likely, and more likely to be accepted, when the people making disciplinary decisions understand not only the organization but the people who compose it. That's why the FBI adjudication process includes experienced special agents and intelligence analysts who have done the work and lived the lives of the employees whose conduct they review. *The FBI Way* calls for compassionate consequences.

WHILE I FOUND COMPASSION PLAYED A SUPPORTING ROLE IN the Bureau's disciplinary process, it was at the core of our relationship with the victims of the crimes we investigated. Still today the FBI's Victim Services Division (VSD) is responsible for ensuring that victims of crimes investigated by the Bureau are provided access to services under the Attorney General Guidelines on Victim and Witness Assistance. The VSD manages the day-to-day operations of the Bureau's Victim Assistance Program (VAP) in all fifty-six field offices and internationally. It places victim specialists in every location across the country to personally assist victims of federal crimes. The VSD also provides training that helps equip FBI personnel to effectively work with victims.

The FBI has several special programs most Americans know little about because, thankfully, most citizens never need these services. But if you did, the FBI victim specialist assigned to your family would become your life raft in a sea of turbulence. For example, the Terrorism and Special Jurisdictions Program provides emergency assistance to injured victims and families of victims murdered in terrorist attacks within the

United States and outside the country, and it serves as a permanent FBI point of contact for terrorism victims.

The Child Pornography Victim Assistance (CPVA) program coordinates assistance and notification services for child victims of pornography and their guardians. Certain federal statutes require law enforcement to notify victims each time images of their victimization are seized as part of an investigation. The amount and frequency of notifications can be overwhelming, especially as victims struggle to cope with the impact of the crime and its aftermath. To help streamline the notification process, CPVA attempts to minimize any additional trauma by limiting unnecessary contact with victims through utilization of a centralized and automated system.

Through this system, the Bureau continues to ensure that victims are advised of the rights and services they are entitled to when any federal cases are opened against offenders found in possession of their images. It doesn't matter how much time has passed since the original exploitation took place. CPVA coordinates throughout the federal law enforcement community and with the National Center for Missing & Exploited Children (NCMEC). During my years of service, I found that the relationship with NCMEC became particularly important when we attempted to determine whether new child porn images depicted a child who had been reported missing.

Compassion also played a central role in advancing our cases as victim services directly supported pending investigations. Interviewing a child is nothing like interviewing an adult. Understanding child brain development during each year of life can be critical to getting an accurate story from a young victim or witness without retraumatizing them. The Child Victim Services Program provides support to child victims and witnesses of federal crimes through investigative forensic interviews and coordination with field specialists. This team is focused on ensuring that any interactions with child victims or witnesses are tailored to the child's stage of development. This approach isn't only compassionate; it is also a smart way to get usable results that stand up in court.

The Bureau doesn't just abandon a person once their case is over. For example, you might want to know that the person who victimized you is about to be released from prison. The FBI partners with the U.S. Attorney's Offices and the Federal Bureau of Prisons in the free, automated Victim Notification System (VNS). Available in English and Spanish, VNS is designed to provide victims with information and notifications regarding their cases. These notifications include information about investigative status, criminal charges filed, outcome of charges, scheduled court proceedings, and whether the offender is being furloughed, released, or has just taken his last breath. I saw firsthand that this continuing dialogue with victims was not only the humane thing to do but a logical extension of the relationship building that was so essential in gaining their trust and cooperation as we developed cases against their offenders. No trust, no cooperation. No cooperation, no case.

I also witnessed the dedicated compassion of our victim

specialists when I was the head of the Cleveland Division. They worked with juvenile prostitutes, treating them not as criminals, but as victims who needed help to escape the trap that they were caught in. For way too long the justice system viewed underage prostitution as a crime problem instead of a compassion problem. It seemed so much easier to arrest a young girl in her early teens, charge her with prostitution, and give her a brief stay in a juvenile lockup, only to have her repeat the cycle all over again. Most of the time, the girl was bonded out of jail by her pimp, who convinced her that he was her boyfriend. So who saved the girl from juvenile limbo every time? The guy who wanted her back in action so he could exploit her every day. She thought he was a hero. Why would she ever cooperate with the police who did nothing more than lock her up? In Toledo, Ohio, the FBI helped change that equation.

In 2003, the FBI launched the Innocence Lost National Initiative to tackle the growing problem of trafficking children for sex in the United States. Since its inception, the effort has recovered or identified almost seven thousand child victims and convicted over twenty-eight hundred of the adults who trafficked them. Courts have sentenced over fifteen of those adults to life sentences, with many of the other adults imprisoned from twenty-five years to life. The program quickly expanded to include almost ninety task forces throughout the country. In 2006, FBI Cleveland's resident agency in Toledo gained approval for its own task force. It became one of the most successful in the nation.

Why would Toledo, Ohio, have a juvenile prostitution problem? Well, as is often the case with complex issues, there were a host of factors. Toledo fell on hard times with the collapse of the industrial economy, the auto industry supply chain, and the resulting impact on the blue-collar workforce. Drug addiction soared as employment bottomed out. Toledo was also the convergence point of interstate highways, railways, and waterways along Lake Erie and the Maumee River. The city was at the crossroads of two of the most traveled interstates in the country, I-80/90 and I-75. Interstate truckers on their way to somewhere else would pull into truck stops for more than just hot coffee and a meal. A large train station there was one of Ohio's busiest passenger rail hubs. And Toledo was just an hour drive from Detroit, with all the crime issues that a larger city can export. A handful of regional pimps were capitalizing on this perfect storm and exploiting the young and vulnerable, not only locally, but across the country. According to the Salvation Army, which worked extensively with sexual exploitation victims, Toledo was ranked the fourth-highest city in the country for sex trafficking arrests and convictions. Experts say about 20 percent of prostitutes are juveniles. Whatever the myriad causes, we had a problem.

The Toledo team, working with our Victim Witness Program, partnered with local nonprofit community groups devoted to rescuing girls who might have lost their innocence, but not their will to survive. (One of those Toledo-based groups would go on to be awarded the FBI Director's Award for Outstanding Community Partnership.) And our talented squad supervisor reached out to local and county law enforcement and proposed trying a different approach to saving not just young girls, but the reputation of the entire city. Everyone was all in. The new strategy meant that girls encountered by the police would be asked two basic questions: "Do you want out?" And "What do you need to make that happen?" The questions were easy, but the answers were a challenge.

According to FBI statistics, the average age a child prostitute fell prey to a pimp was thirteen. The average life expectancy for that child after becoming a prostitute was just seven more years. In Toledo, the girls who eventually said they wanted out, often after multiple encounters with the police and our victim specialists, were taken not to jail, but to one of our nonprofit partners. There they got housing, meals, counseling, and the resources to start on a different path. Most of all, they were treated with compassion, some for the very first time.

Slowly, compassion yielded positive results. As trust was established with these young, hurting kids, they would tell us who their pimps were. They'd also share tales of being transported cross-country and sold for an hour at a time to the mass market of clients at major national events like the Super Bowl. As dozens of victims got the help they needed, the FBI in Toledo got the evidence we needed to put the most brutal of our child traffickers in prison for a long time. Compassion had proven a powerful strategy to combat even the most horrific crime.

—

CLEVELAND'S VICTIM SPECIALISTS ALSO COORDINATED USE of experts on child forensic interviewing when young children had witnessed something no one of any age should ever see.

Jessie Marie Davis, just twenty-six years old, and nearly nine months pregnant, was reported missing from her home in Lake Township, Stark County, Ohio, on June 15, 2007. Jessie's mom, Patricia Porter, found Jessie's two-year-old son, Blake, home alone, a pool of bleach on the bedroom floor, and a bed-side table upside down. The young toddler told his grandma, "Mommy was crying," "Mommy broke the table," and "Mommy's in the rug." The nation's media sensed a gut-wrenching drama unfolding and descended on the bucolic farm fields of Lake Township like an occupying army. The Stark County Sheriff's Department excelled at the two things its citizens asked of them: professionally patrol the roads, and expertly respond to calls for service. But with virtually no homicide experience and the glare of a national spotlight, they would need help.

If local police or sheriffs need a resource or skill set that the FBI has, the Bureau is happy to help. I picked up the phone, called the chief deputy in the county, and asked him how things were going. He said his department was completely consumed by this one case and had already asked the neighboring county for help with road patrol and service calls. I offered potential FBI support with either the crime scene processing or with managing the media. He said yes to both. The chief deputy and I would become partners until this terrible crime got solved.

Jessie Davis was dating Canton, Ohio, police officer Bobby Cutts. Officer Cutts was Blake's father and the father of Jessie's unborn child. At the time Jessie went missing, Cutts was separated from his current wife and had been the subject of domestic abuse and stalking allegations by other women. After a series of FBI supported interviews and polygraphs, Cutts told us where Jessie was. With Cutts riding along in the car, we found Jessie's remains on June 23, 2007, in nearby Summit County, on the edge of Cuyahoga Valley National Park. Now someone had to tell Jessie's family. That task fell to one of FBI Cleveland's victim specialists.

I was there, it was rough, but our victim expert delivered the news quickly and concisely to Jessie's mother and other relatives gathered at a large conference table in a county office. "This is hard news to deliver and hard news to receive," she told the mother. "We've found Jessie." Jessie's mother knew exactly what that meant. There was long, loud sobbing. Even the seasoned agents and deputies in the room teared up. The words no parent wants to hear had been delivered. But the relationship between Jessie's family and the FBI's victim program would continue as long as needed. Compassion may not have directly solved this case, but it did help the victim's family along their path to healing and closure. In this sense, compassion helped fulfill the FBI's broader mission of protecting the well-being of every American.

In February 2008, Cutts was convicted of Jessie's murder and the aggravated murder of her unborn child. He was also guilty of aggravated burglary, gross abuse of a corpse, and child endangering. The court had no compassion for Cutts. He was sentenced to life in prison without eligibility for parole for fifty-seven years.

AS I TOOK ON DIFFERENT LEADERSHIP ROLES OF INCREASING responsibility, overseeing ever-expanding numbers of personnel, I came to view promotions, in part, as an opportunity to help a greater number of employees. I would frequently get questions from agents thinking about entering the management ranks. Inevitably they'd ask whether all the stress of dealing with HQ and being responsible for so many people and programs was worth the minuscule salary increase. First, I'd tell them that if they were going into management for the pay increase, they would be sorely disappointed. Next, I would talk about instinctively knowing when it was time for personal and professional growth, learning to see the Bureau from the thirty-thousand-feet level, and I'd joke a little about living vicariously through everyone else's cases. But I would never end these conversations without talking about "impact." For me, and for most FBI managers, running a squad, a unit, a section, a field office, or an entire FBIHQ division was a chance at having an impact far beyond your own caseload. Besides the obvious impact on a crime problem, a community, or even the country, there was a very real opportunity to make a difference in an FBI employee's life. Compassion was often at the core of this kind of impact.

I shared with younger managers that when I reflected on my own impact, what stood out were the times I was able to use my position to help an employee. Sure, there were important decisions about investigations, authoring major policy changes, fighting for new legislation, winning additional resources, building task forces, and designing training, but the most rewarding impact a leader can have involves people's lives. Truth be told, the FBI hires people who don't need a lot of supervision. Many of the cases I include in this book would probably have happened with or without me. Shoot, maybe some of them happened despite my being in charge.

But while FBI employees don't always need supervision, there are times when they need compassion, and that's when having some rank allows a manager to make a difference. One memorable example came near the start of my management journey, while a second played out near the end.

The role of squad supervisor is an entry-level field office management position. There are layers of field office leadership above you and many layers more back at FBIHQ. You run a squad of agents often dedicated to a single program or purpose, say crimes against children, counterintelligence, cyber crime, or health-care fraud. There might be anywhere from eight to twenty agents, task force officers, and analysts on your squad. Depending on the squad's mission, the agents will be at various points in their careers, some brand-new, many in midcareer, and some about to retire. Your role is important, but it doesn't carry a lot of weight in the overall bureaucracy, so, like most roles, it becomes whatever you choose to make it. I learned that compassion could be a critical asset as a manager.

A squad supervisor needs to advocate for their squad, develop rapport and influence with field office and FBIHQ leaders, implement creative strategies, and generally make things happen by understanding what really matters. I learned you could do this not only in support of the squad's cases but also in support of the squad's people. What's more, I observed the two were inextricably linked: when you compassionately manage your people, you get better operational results.

There was a newer agent in one city I served in, with about two years in, who worked tirelessly and methodically. He developed strong relationships with our police partners, became a valued member of the Evidence Response Team, could always be counted on to deploy at all hours of the night and weekends, and was well on his way to becoming a solid agent. Soon after I took over the squad, I noticed that "Drew" (not his real name) was often the first one in and the last one to leave; I admired his work ethic but wondered about his family. One day he came into my office with a request to take some time off. What would ordinarily be a routine formality became a quest for compassion.

Becoming an FBI agent had been Drew's dream. We all had made sacrifices to achieve our dreams, but Drew's plight seemed perpetual. He was married, had young kids, and had a father who was elderly, extremely frail, and suffering from a debilitating heart condition. None of that would make Drew unusual, except for the fact that Drew was in one city and his family was in another thousands of miles away.

Drew and his wife had decided that Drew would pursue his dream, apply to the Bureau, and, knowing he could be assigned anywhere, Drew would potentially have a costly and long-distance commute. Besides, Drew's wife had a great job that she wanted to keep. What they couldn't have known was that Drew's father would become chronically ill. Now Drew's wife not only was working full-time and caring for the kids, but also had become the caregiver for Drew's ailing father. It was an untenable situation, and the Bureau was in danger of losing a talented agent.

If the Bureau considered everyone's personal and family issues when deciding which field office to assign a new agent, the transfer system would come to a grinding halt. Even for tenured employees, it is extremely difficult to get what is called a "hardship" transfer. Although such transfers happened during my time, I was reminded, in my first of many calls to FBIHQ, that they never happened because of a sick parent: "We all have parents. All of them will get old and sick." "Do you know what it costs to move an agent across the country?" "Having a sick parent is not one of the approved criteria for a hardship transfer." I agreed with everything HQ was telling me. In fact, during the latter half of my career I repeatedly tried to get back home to help care for my parents, but it never happened. I eventually retired and took a corporate security position to get back to Connecticut before my parents passed away. I'm okay with that. Except Drew's case was not about just a sick parent. It was about an entire family making a seemingly ceaseless sacrifice for the Bureau.

The guy I dealt with back at HQ was not a heartless bean-counting bureaucrat. He, too, was an agent, working his way through the management maze, and trying to do the right thing, the compassionate thing. "Show me why this isn't just another sick parent case and we'll consider it," he said. In the interim, he approved some temporary hardship assignments that allowed Drew to work out of the field office nearest his family for a few weeks at a time. But those were just temporary fixes. For the next few months, Drew and I kept feeding his father's entire medical record to HQ. We drafted exhaustive narratives. Each submission would generate even more requests from HQ for further details.

We described the full extent of care Drew's wife was providing for his father. We explained what it cost Drew, a new agent living in one of America's costliest cities, to fly home every month or so. We had doctors document how Drew's father's condition had gotten much worse. And in response to the indelicate but necessary question on everyone's mind, we had the physicians explain that, no, Drew's father was not likely to die anytime soon. His condition was chronic but not terminal. Our persistence paid off. Drew received a permanent transfer back home. The right thing happened, not despite the system, but because the Bureau's system remained open to the human factor. Over thousands of miles, and through the cold concrete of the Hoover building, compassion carried the day. It wasn't just the agent and his family who were the winners here. The Bureau benefited operationally by keeping a talented agent who went on to admirably serve the nation in a host of roles. Compassion was the smart thing to do.

Much later in my leadership experience there was another moment when compassion shined brightly through the FBI's bureaucracy. The Cleveland Division was blessed to have Special Agent Laurie Fournier within its ranks, and I was fortunate to have led that office during Laurie's assignment there. Once you met Laurie you never forgot her. She was one of the most positive and upbeat people most of us had ever met. As described in the Cleveland *Plain Dealer*, "Laurie once turned to an FBI colleague on a case and gushed, 'Isn't fun the best?'" She once danced on bubble wrap at the office, and she sang and played keyboard in an FBI band called Fed Up.

Laurie had been on the health-care fraud squad, then moved on to become training coordinator for agents throughout the Midwest and for local law enforcement leaders. She spent her entire nineteen-year FBI career in the Cleveland office and established deep roots and friendships throughout the community. Fournier had been a social worker before the Bureau, and her compassionate approach was evident when she volunteered to help colleagues deal with personal and professional crises as part of our Employee Assistance Program. As a founding member of Cleveland's evidence team, Laurie spent almost two weeks sifting debris at the nearby Shanksville, Pennsylvania, site where United flight 93 crashed on 9/11.

Laurie was always either finding fun or making it happen, even while she battled cancer. Right up until the last weeks of her life, you would never have known that Laurie was dying. That's because, as I told the *Plain Dealer*, "She wasn't living with cancer, she was living above cancer." And she was still working. Twelve years before her death, Laurie was back home in Upstate New York, where she bumped into a former schoolmate, Mike. They married and soon had two sons, aged nine and six. On December 26, 2009, at a local hospice, Special Agent Laurie Fournier transitioned to her next assignment. She had fulfilled her Bureau mission, but the Bureau's responsibility to Laurie and her family remained.

When an FBI agent dies, someone needs to explain the death benefits to her survivors. Depending on the agent's financial and insurance choices and her designation of beneficiaries, there are any number of policies, programs, and benevolent funds that come into play, including some the agent may never have even known about. Surviving children might be eligible for education grants, and the family often needs immediate help paying for costly funeral expenses. I was aware at the time of Laurie's death that all too often someone handed a grieving family some pamphlets and policy documents, then gave them an FBIHQ phone number to call if they had questions. In my mind, Mike and his kids deserved better than that.

I pored over the legalese in the benefits documents, but despite my law degree, I was still confused. Even if I could explain all the intricacies, I was pretty sure I couldn't answer any detailed questions. I called HQ and told them there had to be a better way. We talked about having a benefits expert on the phone while I visited Mike and the kids at their home. That might work for someone buying auto insurance, but it was too impersonal for a grieving FBI family. I asked if an HQ expert could fly to Cleveland and accompany me to Laurie's house to present the benefits package. By this time in my career I had become accustomed to hearing "We've never done that before," but I had also learned to not accept that answer. An HQ benefits rep agreed to make the trip. It was a tough visit to see Mike and the kids, but it went well, and I couldn't help but think that Laurie was somehow right there in the kitchen with us. More important, I got a call from the HQ specialist after he returned to D.C. The Bureau had decided to make in-person benefits presentations a standard practice. Compassion had been codified.

Laurie would never know this, but the compassionate application of the FBI code wouldn't end with the personalized benefits explanation to her family. Sixteen years after her work at the 9/11 crash site, and eight years after her death, the FBI would determine that Laurie's cancer was linked to her work in Shanksville. The Bureau didn't try to cover up or minimize this. Instead, the FBI brought it out front and center and added a star in Laurie's name to the Wall of Honor. The star was an acknowledgment that she died in the line of duty.

Compassion makes the difference between having a code that flourishes or a code that fails. Your coworkers and teammates may not have to sacrifice their lives for the greater good, but they are giving you their precious time, energy, and talents. If you're entrusted with leadership at any level, you're compelled to lead with compassion. It's not only right, it's smart.

6

CREDIBILITY

C REDIBILITY IS THE CORNERSTONE OF ANY VALUES-based endeavor. And most anything we do that has meaning is rooted in some form of values. So if we want our work not only to succeed but to sustain, people must believe in us and the values we represent. That's as true for the leaders and members of an organization as it is for the organization it-self. Whether we're talking about a company, a community, or a country, it is credibility that determines whether values survive beyond the personalities of individual leaders.

When an organization or its leaders lack credibility, their people never truly assimilate lasting and real values. Dictators force adherence to their rules through fear and intimidation. Cult leaders gain followers who are more loyal to the leader than to any broader value system. That's why cults eventually collapse and dictators are deposed, in part because the only thing they stand for is themselves.

Stephen Miller began as senior adviser to President Trump as a member of his transition team in November 2016 and soon was the architect of an immigration strategy—the separation of migrant parents and children at the border—that shredded the American values embodied by the Statue of Liberty inscription which reads, "Give me your tired, your poor, Your huddled masses yearning to be free, The wretched refuse of your teeming shore. To spread the light of liberty world-wide for every land." In a telling statement, Miller merged his personal allegiance to Trump with loyalty to the nation when he explained the single motivator that makes him tick: "You cannot understand me, you cannot understand anything that I say, do or think if you don't understand that my sole motivation is to serve this president and this country, and there is no other." The heartbreaking result was a policy that was morally reprehensible, incompetently implemented, and illegal. In a word, it was un-American. Miller made the mistake of thinking service to country was the same as service to an individual. When everything you or your organization stands for is more about one person than about a set of values, you're headed for trouble. When that person inevitably falters, your credibility is shot.

Throughout history, entities and empires failed when protecting a person became more important than preserving principles. In contrast, when enlightened process took precedence over personality, values tended to prevail. For example, most

Americans abide by the rule of law not because of loyalty to a person, but because we recognize that laws are put in place for the collective benefit of society. We also generally accept as credible the process by which our laws are enacted and enforced. Police officers read Miranda warnings during custodial interrogations, detectives apply for search warrants and subpoenas, defense counsel is provided for whoever needs it, trial by jury allows the community to weigh the evidence, defendants can testify on their own behalf, and appeals can overturn bad outcomes.

Our justice system hasn't been arbitrary, mysterious, or subject to executive whim. Even when we don't agree with a verdict or a sentence, we find comfort in our belief that the process responsible for how we got there was credible. Certainly, anomalies exist, but the fact that we recognize them as such means we trust our process to get it right most of the time. Transparent process builds credibility, and credibility fosters compliance. Yet, just claiming you have a process isn't enough. Credible preservation of principles happens when the process is codified, objective, and comprehensive. Codification means the process must not only be in writing but also easily accessible, understandable, and taken seriously. In the Bureau, regular surveys ask each employee about the ethics of their leaders, thus sending the message that integrity matters. Some companies, especially small or privately held businesses, pay lip service to employees by essentially asking them to blindly trust that the company has a system in place to deal with wrongdoing.

Those employees quickly conclude that their leadership must not take compliance very seriously. Don't expect employees to trust what they can't see. Trust comes from transparency, and transparency breeds credibility.

"DID YOU SEE THE ONE ABOUT THE MARRIAGE PROPOSAL and the Bureau helicopter?" Anyone wondering whether transparency works ought to hang out near a Bureau watercooler the day after the Office of Professional Responsibility pushes its quarterly report to the field. That's because the Bureau does something few other organizations do: it turns selected disciplinary cases into teachable moments—for everyone. OPR issues brief samplings of certain internal cases that represent troubling trends or serve as reminders of what not to do. These "don't let this happen to you" communications always detail the consequences levied upon the malefactor but strip away identifying details like names and locations. The message is simple—if you act like this, here's what will happen.

It's not only rules and repercussions that should be transparent. People mirror modeled behavior when it's encouraged through positive reinforcement. In the Bureau, exemplary conduct is systematically celebrated. The Manuel J. Gonzalez Ethics Award—named in honor of a respected assistant director who succumbed to cancer at age fifty—is awarded annually to an FBI employee who exemplifies the Bureau's integrity standards. Another honor, the Thomas E. DuHadway Award, given in memory of the beloved and selfless head of the Washington Field Office, regularly recognizes an FBI employee whose concern for colleagues reflects DuHadway's legacy of caring for others without expectation of personal gain.

To celebrate the most exceptional acts—those epitomizing the Bureau motto of Fidelity, Bravery, Integrity—the Bureau instituted an Honorary Medals Program in 1989. The five medals in the program are:

- The FBI Star, awarded for serious injury sustained in the direct line of duty from physical confrontation with criminal adversaries
- The FBI Medal for Meritorious Achievement, awarded for extraordinary and exceptional meritorious service in extreme challenge and great responsibility, including a decisive, exemplary act that results in the protection or the direct saving of life in severe jeopardy in the line of duty
- The FBI Shield of Bravery, presented for brave and courageous acts occurring in the line of duty
- The FBI Medal of Valor, in recognition of an exceptional act of heroism or voluntary risk of personal safety and life, in the face of criminal adversaries
- The FBI Memorial Star, which is presented to a surviving relative where death has occurred in the line of duty as the direct result of adversarial action

In addition to transparent codification, credibility also requires that people believe their organization's process of investigating and adjudicating misconduct is objective, fact-based, and blind to factors like rank, race, religion, gender, age, and orientation. The moment a workforce perceives the process is impacted by external variables is the moment the organization begins to lose both credibility and compliance. This doesn't mean disciplinary decisions shouldn't be attuned to the individuals involved. To the contrary, if consequences track differently for distinct types of people, the process lacks credibility. The one group that merits distinct treatment are the senior leaders. Leaders, in particular, must be expected to model the behavior desired of the larger group. If senior leaders can't comply with standards, then the rank and file won't either. That's why the FBI treats misconduct by senior executives more harshly.

Just ask fired Deputy Assistant Director Peter Strzok.

Strzok, the Bureau's number two counterintelligence official, simultaneously led the inquiry into Hillary Clinton's emails and server during her tenure as secretary of state and the 2016 FBI probe into alleged collusion between the Trump campaign and Russia that eventually led to a special counsel investigation. After appointment of the special counsel, Strzok, a twenty-two-year FBI veteran, supported that office in their inquiry of Russian interference in the presidential election. That is, until a Justice Department inspector general investigation found Strzok had sent anti-Trump texts while helping to run the investigation of Trump and the campaign. The inspector general shared with Special Counsel Robert Mueller that Strzok had exchanged hundreds of biased-looking messages with Lisa Page, a Bureau lawyer with whom he was having an affair. Mueller removed Strzok from the case the next day.

As I made the rounds on various MSNBC shows, the hosts asked what I thought should happen to Strzok. I shared my view that Strzok's judgment, in using FBI devices to exchange highly biased messages with his mistress, was abysmal. His actions, I noted, had caused the public to doubt the objectivity of the Bureau in the Trump/Russia matter; moreover, they could undermine the future effectiveness of the Bureau. I expressed my opinion that Strzok should be, and likely would be, demoted or dismissed. I was thinking beyond this one case, this one president, to the long-term impact of diminished public perception of the FBI as an impartial enforcer of justice. In short, his actions had threatened the Bureau's credibility. I also knew that inside the Bureau, if Strzok's conduct wasn't strongly rebuked, it would be nearly impossible to address similar conduct by lower-ranking employees. In August 2018, Peter Strzok was escorted out of FBIHQ, having been fired by Deputy Director David Bowdich. It was *The FBI Way*.

LAST, ANY PROCESS OF MAINTAINING STANDARDS MUST BE comprehensive. For example, it's not enough to simply establish a way for employees to report integrity concerns if there's no system in place to rapidly respond to and thoroughly investigate their allegations. Employees stop sharing what they know when they think their attempts to do the right thing are falling into a black hole. Similarly, an agency can't say it values fairness and justice if it doesn't offer accused employees a formal opportunity to tell their side of the story, notify them when they're facing serious discipline, and give them a chance to appeal. A complete process should cover the chronology of compliance, from communication of expected standards, to initial reporting of infractions, to investigative protocols, to decision-making about discipline, to employee due process privileges. If one or more of these components is weak, absent, or secret, employee trust erodes and the credibility of the process is compromised.

The FBI has tried to make it as easy as possible to do the right thing. It provides employees and members of the public multiple methods of reporting misconduct concerns. The contact information for OPR, the Inspection Division, the Office of Integrity and Compliance, and the FBI Ombudsman's Office is posted on websites, posters, and documents. Concerns can be reported via phone, email, in writing, and even anonymously. The Bureau tells those who are uncomfortable reporting concerns to the agency that they can directly communicate with the FBI's overseers at the DOJ OIG.

And while I was in the Bureau, when a misconduct allegation came in, we jumped on it.

No one judges the Bureau more harshly than itself. My mentors instilled in me the long-standing precept that the FBI would rather come down hard on its own than have someone else take over the process. We were always mindful that we were one scandal away from the DOJ OIG or congressional oversight committees claiming they could maintain our standards better than we could. That's one reason why the Bureau's internal enforcement mechanism was uncompromisingly meticulous, from the due process provided to employees to how their fates were decided. Yes, external accountability and oversight are critical, but don't ever hand over your values to someone else.

Since credibility demands transparency, FBI employees who become subjects of an internal inquiry are provided formal notice of the investigation, including the nature and details of the allegation and the possible administrative offense codes involved. For example, a notice form might cite offenses such as "Unauthorized Use of a Government Vehicle," or "Inappropriate Relationship with an Informant," or more broadly, "Unprofessional Conduct." If the investigation later identifies additional or more appropriate offenses, a new notice form is issued. Updates on the status of the inquiry are regularly provided to the employee. The initial materials also explain the privileges that can be exercised by the employee, including the ability to be represented by counsel, the right to read the investigative report and submit a written response to it, and in cases involving the most severe discipline, the right to an in-person presentation to the head of OPR.

Even after those privileges are exhausted, an employee

can appeal the final decision, outside of OPR, to the FBI's Human Resources Division. In my experience, this carefully constructed due process was more than just an illusion of fairness; it really did sometimes lead decision makers to alter their initial recommendations. While the Bureau's internal investigative product is reliably accurate, it can't always portray the full picture of the employee and their circumstances. More than one career has been saved after hearing in person from an employee who had been proposed for dismissal. That doesn't mean the process is "soft"; in fact, it is quite the opposite.

Criminals pursued by the FBI have more rights than the agents who target them. For all the built-in process elements, unless the employee is accused of violating the law, their due process privileges never rise to the level of constitutional rights guaranteed to criminals. There is no right to remain silent, no protection against self-incrimination, nor any substantive search and seizure protections where FBI property is concerned. An FBI employee is an open book, subject to urinalysis, polygraphs, and mandatory signed, sworn statements. Failure to fully cooperate with an internal inquiry can result in dismissal. That has to be *The FBI Way* because the public deserves no less from the agency it needs to trust the most.

The credibility of the FBI's process is enhanced by the fact that it keeps internal investigators and adjudicators separate. They are in entirely different units with entirely distinct command chains. This professional distance between fact finders and discipline deciders helps ensure that a dispassionate party decides whether the allegations are proven and what the consequences should be. In addition to comprehensive written investigative reports, a separate adjudication report is prepared setting out the findings of fact, the professional history, performance, and reputation of the accused, and any mitigating or aggravating factors. Unless the recommended discipline is minor, the accused employee is given an opportunity to respond.

While FBI employees are held to excruciatingly high standards, they are also fallible human beings who make mistakes and are expected to learn from their actions. This means not all proven allegations result in discipline. In fact, a substantial percentage of cases during my time in the Bureau ended in either specified "Counseling" of the employee or in an "Oral Reprimand." Neither became a permanent part of the employee's personnel file. The next step up was a formal "Letter of Censure," which was documented in the employee's record. Anything other than minor misconduct raised the likelihood of suspension, which ranged from a few days to a few months without pay. Last, at the extreme end of the discipline spectrum, was dismissal from the rolls of the FBI.

Credibility matters most when the stakes are the highest. The true test of credibility for any internal discipline program is the degree to which it adheres to established process and precedent when imposing its most severe penalty. The Bureau has historically been extremely proficient at maintaining the purity of these decisions, which is why any apparent variance would be glaring, especially if it bore the markers of external political interference. Such was the case of Andy McCabe's firing.

A career special agent for twenty-two years, Andrew McCabe served as the FBI's deputy director, from February 2016 to January 2018. He became acting director following James Comey's firing by President Trump. Once Christopher Wray was named to replace Comey, McCabe returned to the number two role. The DOJ IG found that McCabe improperly disclosed information to the *Wall Street Journal* confirming the existence of an investigation into the Clinton Foundation. The IG concluded McCabe lacked candor in conversations with Director Comey, with the FBI's Internal Investigations Section, and with the IG's office. Jeff Sessions, who was then attorney general, fired McCabe only twenty-six hours before McCabe was eligible to retire and receive his full pension. I have no special knowledge of whether McCabe truly lacked candor with his boss or investigators, or whether his conduct merited dismissal. What I do know is that McCabe's termination lacked the hallmarks of a credible disciplinary decision. That lack of credibility helped to form the basis of McCabe's wrongful termination lawsuit against the DOJ.

In my eyes, the handling of the McCabe matter compromised the credibility of the Bureau's process. During my career, I've convinced employees to retire, placed employees on administrative leave pending retirement, suspended employees right up to their retirement, and told employees they could choose either the dismissal letter in my left hand or their retirement papers in my right hand. But in my twenty-five years of service, with involvement in hundreds of internal inquiries, I have never seen a veteran employee fired within hours of retirement. In this rare instance, political pressure appeared to alter the Bureau's course of consistent application of established processes. Since credibility and consistency are joined at the hip, where one is absent, the other fails. That's why doing the right thing when it matters most and the pressure is painful can make the difference between credibility and corruption.

DOING WHAT'S RIGHT WHEN YOU KNOW IT WON'T BE POPU-lar is a necessary component of leading in the FBI. A common sentiment in the FBI goes something like "If you go your whole career without ever being investigated by OPR, you haven't really done your job." Somehow I thought that would never apply to me—until Miami.

Augusto Guillermo "Willie" Falcon and Salvador Magluta were major Cuban American drug smugglers with connections to the Panamanian president Guillermo Endara, who established thirty-three shell companies for the two kingpins. According to the DEA, in their heyday, Falcon and Magluta controlled the largest drug ring on the East Coast, and one of the five biggest in the world. Friends since high school, the pair smuggled seventy-five tons of cocaine into the United States in the 1980s. When they were arrested in October of 1991, federal law enforcement identified $2.1 billion in assets the two men controlled in South Florida. Falcon and Magluta were violent and ruthless, and their approach to life didn't end when they were arrested. Their organization threatened the lives of federal agents. At least five key witnesses in their trial were mercilessly shot, three fatally, throughout the Miami area.

Even the family members of key witnesses were shot in attempts to silence the witnesses. A rooftop sniper in Miami killed one man and critically wounded two others, including the brother of a vital prosecution witness who had survived an earlier shooting. Falcon and Magluta's former lawyer, Juan Acosta, had been gunned down so he wouldn't become a government witness. Falcon's own wife, Alina, was shot repeatedly in the face as she left a Coral Gables beauty parlor.

Witnesses who weren't killed were paid for their silence. Meticulous records kept by Magluta revealed that at least three witnesses accepted cash in return for either not testifying or changing their stories. They hired an all-star legal team to battle the monumental drug case assembled by federal investigators and prosecutors. Yet, despite the demise of key witnesses, the case against the pair was believed to be so solid and so significant that Kendall Coffey, the U.S. attorney for the Southern District of Florida, decided he would handle the trial himself. That decision ultimately led to the end of Coffey's career as a prosecutor.

Unbeknownst to Coffey or anyone on the prosecution

team, Falcon and Magluta's organization had identified the jurors and determined which of them were susceptible to bribery. Between their legal defense and payoffs to the jurors, the two defendants doled out about $24 million. On February 17, 1996, the jury foreman announced that the jury had found Falcon and Magluta innocent of their drug charges. The crowded courtroom was shocked. A despondent Coffey adjourned to the Lipstik "gentlemen's club" to drown his sorrow. What happened next was unclear, but after a dispute with a dancer in the club, rumors and allegations quickly swirled in the legal and law enforcement community that Coffey had bitten the stripper. Coffey was summoned to then attorney general Janet Reno's office in Washington. He announced his resignation the next day.

In the FBI, witness- and jury-tampering investigations are generally worked by public corruption squads, regardless of the nature of the underlying offense. Public corruption is part of the FBI's White-Collar Crime Program, and in 1999, I became head of Miami's White-Collar Crime Branch, with oversight of the tampering and obstruction cases against Falcon and Magluta. Bienvenidos a Miami; welcome to Miami. Miami's public corruption agents were among the best in the Bureau. They kept me briefed on significant progress they were making to unravel precisely how the drug organization had funded and carried out the shootings and executions of witnesses and the bribing and threatening of jurors. It wasn't easy.

Methodically, the investigative team recruited new informants and even developed information on houses where the organization might have secreted millions of dollars in cash. The agents developed probable cause to search those locations, partnered with a respected assistant U.S. attorney (AUSA) to draft affidavits, and appeared before a federal magistrate who signed multiple search warrants. An air of anticipation started to spread among our corruption agents.

Extensive planning always precedes FBI searches. Since this search involved suspected stash houses where a violent international drug organization might have stored drugs and dollars, the planning was even more detailed than usual. Safety was always priority one, so we initiated extensive surveillance on each location to determine whether the sites were occupied and by whom. The talented FBI Miami ERT was told to prepare for potentially intensive and even "destructive" searches. The division's SWAT team began planning for breaching multiple, potentially fortified, dwellings. The office operations center activated its staffing plan. A comprehensive written operations plan was drafted covering contingencies and naming each of the dozens of employees from all over the office selected for the operation and their specific roles. Except there was one contingency the plan didn't yet address—success.

After I read the first draft of the plan, I asked a simple question: "What if we're successful?" In other words, what if, even after a decade, the organization still had millions in cash sitting at these sites? Which agents would take custody of it? How would we securely transport it through the streets of Miami? Where, how, and who would accurately count that much money, and, would we just lock it in the evidence room? These weren't just logistics questions, they went directly to ensuring a successful prosecution by protecting our credibility.

The AUSA assigned to this case was a highly experienced pro who had been the prosecutor in the federal trial of ex-Panamanian dictator Manuel Noriega. He was seasoned, smart, and serious. He knew whatever we found in those searches, perhaps ledgers, photographs, dope, cash, or even corpses, would be challenged in court by the slickest defense lawyers that drug money could buy. Any FBI employees who found pertinent evidence might have their work product, technique, and integrity attacked. The AUSA discussed with me his desire for a search plan that could withstand the strongest challenges in court. He noted that the burden of proof would be on the government to show that any cash found during the searches dated back to the Falcon–Magluta era and had been under their control. The prosecutor and I pondered whether the FBI lab, in addition to determining the age of the money, might be able to demonstrate how long it had been stored in a specific place based on mold, mildew, or natural degradation within whatever packaging and environment we found it. We even talked about the possibility of recovering fingerprints or hair and fiber evidence off either the money or its packaging that might be attributed to organization associates. The credibility of our case depended on getting the details right.

Since any money discovered in the searches might have forensic value, we included in the ops plan any contingency and concerns we could imagine related to seizing sizable sums of cash. The SAC, a veteran troubleshooter, suggested we borrow an armored car from a cooperative cash hauler and assign a lead vehicle and a follow car staffed with SWAT operators. We designated agents by name on each of the search teams to take custody and control of any cash. We decided to forgo any attempt to count the money in the office with our old and sometimes inaccurate counting machines. Instead, we would enter any bulk cash into evidence, seal it, then transport it to our local bank for an accurate and monitored count. The ops plan specified that any cash or packaging might be subject to forensic examination and should be kept undisturbed.

The written plan was emailed to each of the dozens of search team participants, then printed out and handed to each member, then verbally detailed at an "all hands" briefing the day before the search warrant executions. What wasn't included in the written plan was the old Yiddish proverb "Man plans, God laughs."

The searches kicked off in the early morning. About an hour into the operation a call came in from one of the search teams. The attic of one of the houses contained a lot of cash. I got on the phone with the supervisor at that site and asked him to estimate the amount of cash. He said the team's consensus was that they were looking at millions of dollars. I asked him to ensure the chain of custody remained limited to only the designated "cash agents" and told him that the armored car was on its way. He assured me the plan was being followed.

The armored car and its escort vehicles pulled into the back lot of the FBI Miami Field Office. The SAC and I moved outside just as the back door of the armored carrier was unbolted and swung open by a SWAT agent. Inside the back of the truck, on this sweltering sauna of a Miami day, were two very proud and perspiring agents who had just found the most money they had ever seen in their relatively young lives. In fact, they were so happy and eager to show their bosses the fruits of their labor that they were "making it rain" inside that truck. Loose bills were cascading from the agent's hands in a shower onto the floor of the vehicle. The boss and I gave each other a look. *Man plans, God laughs.* I asked the agents to take a break for a moment while the SAC and I talked about next steps.

I reminded the boss that the money had potential forensic value, but that more important, the AUSA expected every aspect of our operation, including the agents involved, to be attacked in court. The boss and I conferred about how best to insulate the agents from allegations of theft, since they were literally sitting in loose cash. I also noted that our ops plan was discoverable by the defense, who might try to undermine chain of custody by hammering the agents for personally handling and "playing" with the money. The boss gave it a few moments and told me he thought the best damage control for the agents and the operation would be to have a male manager discreetly take the two male agents into the men's locker room and have them searched to demonstrate they had no money on them. I agreed.

The SAC summoned over my counterpart, who headed the office's National Security Branch and could serve as a neutral and disinterested party to document that the agents were "clean." When the boss explained what needed to be done, my colleague wasn't pleased with his assignment. But after hearing the issues, he understood. I explained to the agents what would happen and why. Neither of them posed any objection. My colleague escorted them to the locker room, where the agents disrobed enough to allow the manager to say that all the cash was still in the armored car. We documented our precautionary measures and thought we had put our concerns to rest. Yet our efforts to preserve the credibility of our case would soon be called into question.

The SAC and I spent the next year of our careers under OPR inquiry. A few days after the search warrants, supervisors in the office gave me a heads-up that the rumor mill was getting out of control with talk that the boss and I had agents "strip-searched" because we "didn't trust our agents." The rumors reached FBIHQ, and an internal inquiry was launched that fly-specked every facet of our ops plan and our decision-making. Agents, supervisors, prosecutors, and finally, the SAC and I were all interviewed.

The process was painfully long, and the irony was not lost on me that a former OPR unit chief was now in the subject line of an internal investigation. *The FBI Way* meant that no one at any level was above scrutiny or beyond learning a lesson. When it came time for my interview, I defended my thought processes to the investigators. The SAC and I could have done the easy thing in that rear parking lot and risked jeopardizing evidence in a major case. Instead we chose to protect the investigation and the reputation of the two agents despite the risk of office perceptions. I believed in what I was saying.

But I also asked myself what I could have been done better. Despite written plans and verbal briefings, if the search team that found the cash didn't seem to understand what to do with it, I hadn't effectively communicated. If the agents who were searched in that locker room might not have fully understood why that had to happen, I hadn't made it clear. After one year of inquiry, a letter from FBIHQ arrived at my desk. The short document advised that the inquiry was closed with no findings of misconduct or need for discipline. It suggested something that the SAC and I already knew: that communications were at the root of office misperceptions about what happened the day of the searches. It was a hell of a way to learn an obvious lesson about communication and credibility.

THE FBI BANKS ON ITS CREDIBILITY. I DEPENDED ON IT EVery time I slipped my credentials out of the front left breast pocket of my suit, flipped open the leather case, and displayed those three bright blue letters with my photo beneath them. In fact, the words *credibility* and *credentials* have similar Latin roots. The word *credentials*, defined as "a qualification, achievement, personal quality or aspect of a person's background, typically when used to indicate that they are suitable for something," has its roots in the medieval Latin *credentia*, which means "giving credence to, recommending." The word *credibility* is from the Latin *credibilis*, derived from *credere*, which means to believe. The importance of the public's belief in the credibility of those creds, the item carried by all FBI agents, becomes apparent the first time you flash them, as well as the rare instance when they aren't respected.

I was about two years into my assignment in Atlanta when FBIHQ received solid intel that there was going to be a "hit" on an Indian official who was visiting friends in Atlanta. The VIP was a Sikh leader who helped broker a short truce between the Indian government and Sikh militants. Apparently, the Sikh militants didn't like him. The FBI isn't an agency that provides protection to visiting dignitaries, but this was now a terrorism threat, and we didn't much care for international assassinations in the Peach State. I was part of a round-the-clock security detail protecting the official. On the last day of the detail, when our visitor was scheduled to fly back home out of Atlanta-Hartsfield Airport, we learned the assassin was in Atlanta. He was going to be on the same flight as the VIP. According to our source, we were now looking for a man in a saffron-colored turban.

I was already on my way to the airport to serve as the advance agent well ahead of the rest of our team's arrival with the dignitary. Our squad supervisor relayed the intel to me and told me to pick up speed, get through the international terminal, find the gate area, and let him know if I spotted someone with a saffron turban. He said that he and the rest of the squad were headed my way to back me up. I badged my way through security at the International terminal, then found the gate for our guy's Lufthansa flight connecting through Germany. I breathed a sigh of relief as I scanned the passengers already seated in the waiting area and found no one wearing anything remotely resembling a turban. I radioed back to my supervisor, "So far, so good." My assessment was premature, and the credibility of my FBI credentials was about to be tested.

Soon after my optimistic report to the boss, a man in a bright orange-yellow turban strolled to the gate. He was followed by two more guys with the same headwear. They were trailed by four more gentlemen with similar colored cloth wrapped around their noggins. That made seven potential Sikh assassins and one FBI agent, which sounded like pretty good odds to my twenty-eight-year-old brain. I radioed my boss. Since there might be kids reading this book, I won't bother repeating what he said. As you might imagine, he was a bit animated. My supervisor instructed me to find the Lufthansa terminal manager and tell him the flight was going to be delayed. By now passengers were preboarding.

I approached the gate agent, discreetly gave him a peek at my creds, and asked to speak with the terminal manager. While we waited what seemed like an eternity for the Lufthansa supervisor to show up, more passengers streamed onto the flight. Finally a stereotypically blond, tall, impeccably dressed German fellow appeared, looked down at me, and asked in an annoyed-sounding German accent, "What's the problem?" I asked if we could go somewhere more discreet to talk. He said no. I flashed him the creds, explained that we had a threat to the safety of his aircraft and to the passengers on it, and informed him we would need to delay the flight. He asked how long. I told him it would take however long we needed to interview several passengers and search all their luggage. In his thick accent, the manager proudly informed me that "We have a perfect on-time record on this flight, this flight is never late, and it won't be late tonight." My credibility test was coming.

"Either you get the captain out of the cockpit or I'll get him myself—it's your choice," I explained. This was eleven years before the 9/11 attacks and there was no telling whether a captain was going to understand why he should listen to the concerns of a sole FBI agent, but it was the logical next step. The terminal manager harrumphed, turned toward the jet bridge, and returned with the captain. By now most of the passengers had boarded. I was still waiting for my reinforcements to make their way through Atlanta traffic. The captain and I went off to a corner, where I showed him my creds. I explained that we had a legitimate threat to the life of someone on this aircraft and had reason to believe the threat might play out while the plane was in flight. I told him we needed to deplane the passengers, conduct interviews, and search the luggage. "Okay, you're the boss," the captain replied with his own German inflection.

I had just stopped a loaded commercial airliner from taking off. Those three bright blue letters on my FBI credentials had passed the credibility test.

The supervisor and my squad mates rolled into the gate area like the cavalry. They brought a U.S. Customs supervisor with them and deposited our Indian official in a holding room. Customs agreed to pull all the checked bags out of the cargo hold, open and search them, and run their bomb dogs past everything. In addition, each passenger was told to come off the plane with their carry-on bags, which all got the same treatment as the stowed luggage. We ran every name on the flight manifest through all the databases. We separately interviewed each of the saffron-topped travelers, who all had legitimate travel documents and reasons for travel. We had a plane full of unarmed, nonviolent saints. We also had a duty to warn our protectee of the intelligence we possessed. The flight was safe, but he was not.

Our friend shrugged his shoulders. After we suggested that he rethink his plans to go back to India, he expressed a fatalistic sentiment: if he died, he died; when it was his time to go, there would be nothing he could do about it. He survived the trip, and he made it back home safely. The FBI had done its job. But his time came not long after he settled in back in India, where he and his security guards were shot and killed while traveling in a car. The official did have a point. You can't possibly prevent every bad thing from happening. Yet the FBI relies so absolutely on its credibility that it toils mightily to thwart anything that threatens to undermine it. Sometimes that threat can't be stopped, and sometimes the danger is deadly. That was the peril posed by Robert Hanssen, one of our own.

ONE OF THE REASONS THE FBI REMAINS CREDIBLE IS ITS track record of investigating its own, admitting its mistakes, sucking it up, and fixing whatever the hell happened. The Bureau doesn't cover it up or sugarcoat it; they deal with it. That's true even when the details are devastatingly horrific. It was true even when the facts were so bad that when I heard them on the car radio, I considered pulling over on the Florida Turnpike to avoid hitting another car. It was true even when I just heard on the news that my very first headquarters unit chief spent the last two decades spying for the Russians. It was February 20, 2001, and I was halfway to my office at FBI Miami.

"Possibly the worst intelligence disaster in U.S. history." That's what the Department of Justice said following the espionage arrest of Robert Philip Hanssen. My old boss, "Bob," is now serving fifteen consecutive life sentences without parole at the "supermax" federal prison in Colorado. The only reason Hanssen wasn't executed was that he agreed to completely cooperate in the damage assessment because he wanted his wife to get a widow's portion of his pension. Hanssen started betraying his country when he offered himself to the Russian intelligence services back in 1979, just three years after joining the FBI.

Over the years, Hanssen gave thousands of highly classified documents to the Russians in return for almost $1.5 million in cash and diamonds. He handed the adversary America's nuclear war plans, and new military weapon designs, and gave up a gold mine of counterintelligence operations, including the location of an FBI tunnel underneath the Soviet embassy in Washington. Most disturbing of all, Hanssen revealed the names of Russian intelligence officers secretly working for the United States. This bastard was responsible for the Russians executing as many as ten of our best human sources.

During his entire time as a spy, Bob remained anonymous to the Russians; they never figured out the identity of their biggest asset. And for far too long, he remained a mystery to the growing but determined team of FBI and CIA counterintelligence operators secretly assigned to find and stop him. It turns out Hanssen was spying for the Russians while CIA officer Aldrich Ames was doing the same thing. But once Ames was arrested and debriefed, there were still intelligence losses that couldn't be explained. These included an abrupt end to the FBI case against State Department official Felix Bloch when the Russians suddenly broke contact with him. So a special team was quietly formed to ferret out whoever it was that was still hurting us. I was a young supervisor at FBIHQ when some of my more experienced colleagues started disappearing to work off-site on a "special project." They were hunting for Bob, but they just didn't know it yet.

The Hanssen story became the subject of books, movies, and TV shows. His childhood, his relationship with his father, his finances, his sex life, and his ties to Opus Dei Catholicism have all been scrutinized by psychologists, profilers, and spy catchers. Each of us who directly worked for Bob were interviewed at length as part of an attempt to piece together the warning signs and indicators that were missed. Each of us has our own tales of the odd, almost Asperger-like qualities of the strange man we worked for. But as I was being debriefed by investigators, long after Hanssen's arrest, I had a chilling revelation. This guy coughed up my own double agent operation. Let me explain.

Making life miserable for foreign intelligence officers posted to the United States is part of the unofficial job description of an FBI counterintelligence agent. If you can stymie their operations, flip their sources, eavesdrop on every facet of their lives, and recruit their wife and their mistress, you will tie them into a knot that can't be undone. If you do that across the country, you can essentially render ineffective an entire foreign intelligence service. That's where double agent operations (DA ops) come in. The general idea is to find just the right cooperator, usually a true patriot up for an adventure, get them next to a known foreign intelligence officer, have the cooperator offer their services to that target, and watch the fun begin.

The bad guys know that this American soldier, sailor, defense contractor, scientist, or business executive might be working for the FBI, or, then again, she might not be. That $100 bill on the sidewalk might be counterfeit or attached to a string, but what if it's not? Sometimes the foreign spy bites because he simply can't resist whatever military, economic, or diplomatic secrets our asset can access. When that happens, and he starts tasking our asset, we get to learn exactly what a country is shopping for, what they might already have, and how and where they meet and communicate with sources. If all goes well, the other team starts paying our asset, and we sit back and collect our adversary's cash. In really special cases, we can use DA ops to pass what's called "disinformation"—maybe a faulty design for a military weapon that will take them years to discover doesn't work. Imagine during wartime, passing the enemy our "secret" battle plan that, if they believe it to be credible, causes them to march right into our hands. This stuff happens. I've been there, done that.

In my early field office days, I developed the makings of a pretty decent DA op. It's all classified, but the other side bought it, hook, line, and sinker. I even got to brief Colin Powell on it. Well, one day my operation stopped dead in its tracks. The other side told our asset in no uncertain terms that they would never meet again. Done. Over. Finished. We all wondered what had happened. Experiencing this kind of success only to have it come to a crashing halt started me wondering whether I needed a change. Atlanta offered a good-size playing field, but maybe the bigger picture at FBIHQ might allow me to learn more about the global counterintelligence game. I was a little young to be putting in for promotion to HQ, but I gave it a shot. I applied for an opening in the Counterintelligence Division. My phone rang several weeks later. It was a manager named Bob Hanssen. He had picked me for a job in his newly formed unit. Lucky me.

It all clicked when, years later, the Hanssen debriefers hinted to me that he had exposed quite a few DA ops. I let them know that soon after I arrived at HQ, Hanssen let slip that he had remotely admired my fieldwork by scrolling through my Atlanta files in the automated case system. I took this to mean that Bob was just checking me out before promoting me. Now I wondered how much the Russians paid him for my case. In fact, most of my fellow supervisors in Bob's unit had previous success against the Russians. Here's the thing, though—Bob's new unit wasn't about Russia at all. It was a new economic espionage unit looking at nontraditional threats. So why did Bob pick us? I'm convinced it was one of three possibilities. Either Hanssen, in some perverse sense of guilt, felt he owed something to the agents whose operations he sold for cash, or he was impressed that we damaged the adversary he was working for, or he simply wanted to keep a close eye on those of us whose cases he had burned. Regardless, I finally knew what happened to my op. It was enough to make me question the credibility of what we did and how we operated.

Why did I include the Hanssen debacle in a chapter called "Credibility"? After all, not only did the Bureau make a huge mistake in hiring this traitor, but it then failed to act on alarm bells when they started ringing. Hanssen had six kids. The kids all attended expensive private schools. His wife was a teacher's aide. He earned the moderate government salary of a mid-level manager. How was he affording all this? To make matters worse, Hanssen's brother-in-law, also an FBI agent, reported that Bob had a stack of cash on his dresser and should be scrutinized for possible espionage. It gets worse. While Hanssen was betraying the nation, he waltzed into his section chief's office and plunked down a classified report he had hacked from his boss's computer. Bob claimed he was merely proving the system had security flaws, but he was likely covering his ass. But, again, what's this have to do with the FBI's credibility?

Credibility isn't about being perfect, it's about being trusted. Trusted to do the right thing even when it's painful. Once it became clear there was a mole inside the intelligence community, the Bureau led the hunt for whoever it was, wherever they might find him. Mole hunts aren't pretty; suspects' lives get turned upside down. The FBI's spy catchers prayed that their target wouldn't be one of their own. They tore through potential suspects at all agencies. For a while they were convinced it was someone at CIA. That was ugly. But when the hard-earned evidence pointed to Hanssen, they descended on him. Hanssen was arrested at gunpoint on a cold February morning in 2001 near his home in Vienna, Virginia, right after he laid down his last cache of classified material at a dead drop site in a park. Now the Bureau's work was just beginning.

When about a day passed without a Russian showing up to service Hanssen's dead drop, FBI director Louis Freeh issued a press release. There was no cover-up, no minimizing the mistakes, no excuses. This was our disaster, we owned it. The Bureau would publicly take its lumps. More important, it was time to inspect the damage and plug the holes that led to the deadliest breach in the agency's history. To regain the public's trust, the repair work would have to be as visible as the video of agents handcuffing Hanssen. Being credible is painful sometimes.

I'll spare you the minutiae of every single new, improved, or simply stepped-up security measure that resulted from Hanssen. Congressional oversight committees were briefed on all the painstaking details. For one, the FBI's internal Security Division was permanently enhanced. Every year, employees complete a daunting form demanding the smallest detail of their family finances. Financial analysts pore over how much an employee's household is taking in and how much money is flowing out. Mortgage debt, auto loans, tuition payments, and home equity loans are matched against all salaries, rental property incomes, gifts and inheritances. What does your spouse earn? What are the VIN numbers on all your cars? The whole point is not only to identify unexplained wealth, but to determine if someone with a Top Secret clearance is in over their heads and becoming vulnerable. And there is more.

Every five years, like clockwork, each FBI employee undergoes a complete reinvestigation as if they are being hired all over again. Neighbors, coworkers, and the local police are questioned. Employees are interviewed at length about their reported foreign travel, and every page of their passports is checked for any unreported travel. Foreign contacts are listed and explained, including relatives and friends abroad. When I was AD, my list of foreign contacts was a long one. It was my job to meet and socialize with the Brits, the Aussies, the Kiwis, and the Canucks. I also had numerous and sensitive sit-downs with foreign intelligence officers from a host of nations as operations required. Had I ever passed classified intel to a foreigner? Yes, of course. All that had to be explained. Next comes a polygraph exam that includes countermeasures aimed at catching anyone trying to beat the machine. If you make it through that process, you are good for a while, or at least until a possible random urinalysis or polygraph. If things don't go well, your life gets complicated. That's how the Bureau helps maintain its credibility. But the Bureau isn't like other components of our government.

Politicians and presidents would run out of their shoes screaming bloody murder if anyone suggested they undergo anything like the Bureau regimen. Even your local police department would find themselves up to their neck in privacy lawsuits and union grievances if they tried this kind of personnel security protocol. Yet, credibility is costly, and the Bureau's mission is way too important to leave to chance. If enough people lose trust in an elected official, that official gets impeached or voted out. But we don't have another FBI. There's nothing else like this bedrock institution. That's why its credibility is critical. The nation's security demands it, and the Bureau's mission depends on it.

Whether it is a single employee going bad or the entire agency's credibility under fire, there is more than just the FBI's national security mission at stake. Every facet of the Bureau's responsibilities would suffer if sources decided they couldn't place their careers, and even their lives, in the hands of that FBI agent sitting across the table. The same is true for the general public. When an agent pulls out their creds and asks someone to do the right thing by talking about what they saw, heard, or know, it is the whole Bureau standing at their door. If that citizen doubts that they can trust the FBI to be better than the person under investigation, the system fails. That's why credibility plays a particularly pivotal role in the Bureau's ability to nail powerful but corrupt politicians, officials, and cops.

No agency beats the FBI in the fight against public corruption. Whether it's the local dogcatcher, the mayor, governor, congressional member, or the president of the United States, when a government official betrays their office, they are betraying the public trust. Successful public corruption cases have sweeping and lasting impact on a community. Ridding the system of one or two bad apples stops the rot from infecting the whole barrel and restores faith in the process. And longer-term pervasive corruption by elected and appointed officials doesn't merely undermine our system. Eventually, their corruption becomes the system. I discovered that in the county where Cleveland, Ohio, sat, the system was rotting from the inside out, and the stink was getting on everyone.

SUCCESSFUL CORRUPTION CASES ARE MADE WITH INFOR-mants and wires. These cases are tough because citizens who want to do the right thing fear retribution by people with power and rank. That was true whether we were investigating a shady zoning official or a dirty police officer. These cases didn't just fall into our lap. Even when someone approaches the FBI, usually because they can no longer stand the personal or professional toll of paying bribes or doing favors to get something done, you can't take their word for it. There has to be additional evidence. That's where the Bureau is at its best: developing more sources, sifting through mounds of records, following a money trail, and putting enough evidence together to convince a judge to order wiretaps. Sources are particularly difficult to develop, maintain, and control.

In my time, I learned that informants often came with their own baggage. They might have had criminal records, or they might be so afraid of the consequences of cooperating against perceived power that they wouldn't testify in court. Of course, that wasn't an issue with audio, video, and undercover agents. Those more sophisticated investigative techniques worked well for us in the case of the crooked commissioner of Cuyahoga County.

Jimmy Dimora ran Cuyahoga County like a crime family. He served as county commissioner from 1998 until 2010, and for most of that time was chairman of the county's Democratic Party. Before that, Dimora had been mayor of Bedford Heights for seventeen years. That was a long time for the citizens of the greater Cleveland area to put up with Dimora's bribe demands, shakedowns, and lining his pockets with taxpayer dollars. Finally, some of them decided they wouldn't take it anymore.

When I reported for duty as head of the FBI in northern Ohio, I wondered, *Why isn't Cleveland thriving? Where's the economic surge of new businesses, hotels, and residences that should be found in any place with a long beautiful shoreline, close-in suburbs with superb schools, professional football, basketball, and baseball teams, the largest theater district outside of New York, and a health-care network anchored by the famous Cleveland Clinic?* People I encountered just shrugged their shoulders and cited everything from cold weather to the demise of the auto and steel industries as reasons why the town still couldn't shake its old reputation as "the mistake on the lake." All those obstacles and more were valid excuses for Cleveland's stagnation. But as our public corruption squad agents began to brief me on their cases, I learned there might be more going on.

Our case started small, within the city, but slowly grew into an avalanche of allegations blanketing the county. Frustrated business owners and developers were growing tired of having to bribe Cleveland's building inspectors to get anything done. An undercover agent posing as a real estate developer started paying bribes to one city inspector after another. Agents flipped one of those bad inspectors and convinced him to solicit a bribe from a big construction executive we knew was dirty. Sure enough, the bigwig slipped the inspector some cash. When we immediately arrested our target in the parking lot outside, he said, "You don't want me, you want Dimora and

Russo and them." The case had just moved from city building inspectors to the top of the county government.

The second-most-populated county in Ohio was run by three elected commissioners. The trio each independently ruled as they saw fit. County hiring decisions were up to them, which opened the floodgates to patronage, no-show jobs for friends and relatives, and plenty of corruption. Big money contract awards for paving county roads, fixing bridges, building or refurbishing county office complexes, janitorial services, plowing the snow, or mowing the grass on county land—all had to get the thumbs-up from the commissioners. And a thumbs-up from Dimora cost money.

Dimora, morbidly obese, loved fine dining. He just didn't like paying for his meals. He was particularly fond of thick steaks and Crown Royal whisky. When he and his criminal cohort, county auditor Frank Russo, would hit places like Delmonico's in Independence, Ohio, Dimora would order the twenty-three-ounce cowboy steak for himself. Dinner tabs of $3,000 or $4,000 weren't unusual, because, why not? They weren't paying. We were all paying the price.

Anyone naive enough to honestly pursue a county contract, job, or favor was going to either pay or go home. Cash was often slid under the table toward Dimora in envelopes as thick as the steaks on the diners' plates. Occasionally an employee on the county payroll would have to cover the tab out of gratitude for their job, or they'd figure out how to stick the taxpayers with the bill. Dimora and Russo referred to their check payers as "sponsors," as in, "Hey, Frank, who's our sponsor tonight?"

Dinners weren't the only perk sponsors were paying for. Lavish excursions to Las Vegas and Canada featured all-expense-paid stays at top resorts and casinos, including prostitutes handpicked for Dimora. FBI surveillance teams covered the commissioner on one of these "gift" trips to Vegas and photographed him at a "clothing optional" resort. Mercifully, Jimmy kept his swim trunks on.

By this time, our office had electronically surveilled Dimora and other county players for a while. A federal judge signed off on multiple wiretap applications and closely monitored our progress. As I studied the transcripts of Dimora's corrupt phone conversations, I couldn't help but wonder if I was reading a script from a lost episode of *The Sopranos*. From what we were hearing, our county had become a de facto organized crime syndicate. As the list of officials under investigation kept growing and the number of wiretaps increased, the case consumed our corruption squad and began to swallow the whole office.

The case touched on so many aspects of county life and involved so many big-name business interests that our new U.S. attorney, Steve Dettelbach, a man of integrity, immediately announced he was recusing himself before even picking up the case file. The law firm Steve was coming from had some connection to a potential part of the investigation, and Dettelbach didn't want any appearance of conflict to derail this massive operation. The recusal was hard for Steve, a committed corruption prosecutor. But that's how credibility is maintained. Steve asked the U.S. attorney in nearby Detroit to take responsibility for approving anything that required high-level sign-off. That U.S. attorney, Barbara McQuade, graciously agreed and came down to Cleveland for a briefing. Barbara was supersharp and quickly grasped the complexities of the case. (Ten years later, we found ourselves working together as television news analysts, commenting about an even higher level of corruption—the presidential kind.)

Criminal wiretaps are resource intensive. Unlike some national-security-related eavesdropping under FISA, criminal wires require round-the-clock shift work to listen to each call in real time. We started pulling in retirees, agents, and trusted task force officers from other squads just to monitor the court-ordered coverage. But I was developing another concern; we had numerous corruption cases beyond Dimora's circle that needed to be investigated. I sought and received FBIHQ approval to create a second corruption squad and name an additional supervisor. Our efforts to restore credibility to county government eventually paid off.

In July 2008, well over one hundred agents and evidence techs from the FBI and IRS fanned out across the Cleveland area armed with search warrants for government offices, businesses, and homes. News crews raced to multiple sites around town and captured images of agents carting out hard drives, boxes, and files. The county's pay-to-play culture was being exposed for all to see. The stranglehold of corruption that had choked Cuyahoga County began to loosen. But it would take over two more years of intense investigative work by superstar agents and analysts before anyone could come up for air. The citizens of the Cleveland metro area never expressed doubt about what the FBI was doing; in fact, they cheered. At a restaurant one night, two local citizens who recognized me approached my family and simply said, "Thank you."

The very public execution of search warrants caused many of the corrupt politicians, officials, and vendors to panic. Within twenty-four hours of the searches, a major cooperator came forward and confessed that he was a middleman for bribes and a witness to the paid trips, the parties with hookers, and the extravagant dining provided for Dimora by people seeking to do business with the county. The source provided details of how he passed Dimora money from a prominent local attorney to influence the commissioner's decision to buy a large downtown bank complex for use as county offices. The purchase of that property and a host of legal issues around it cost county taxpayers more than $45 million. Now it was Dimora's turn to pay.

"Where's Figliuzzi? He has a hard-on for me." That was Dimora, in the underground garage at FBI Cleveland getting fingerprinted and photographed. The county commissioner had refused to resign from office despite being under federal investigation. In fact, he publicly and defiantly challenged prosecutors to either indict him or move on. The grand jurors, all county citizens, were happy to oblige. Dimora was arrested at his home on September 15, 2010. And yes, if Dimora's comment about me meant that FBI agents pursue corrupt politicians with a passion, he was right.

When the investigation finally ended, and all the defendants had their days in court, more than seventy officials, including two county judges, government employees, contractors, business leaders, bagmen, and drivers, were convicted. Among them was the county auditor, Frank Russo, who was sentenced to twenty-two years but eventually flipped on Dimora to earn a sentence reduction. After reviewing years of county contract awards and vendor records, and evidence gathered via subpoenas, cooperators, and wiretaps, we couldn't help but wonder if there were any major county contracts that weren't tainted by corruption.

We may never know how much the Cleveland area's economy was stymied by the personal greed of immoral, unethical leaders. But undoubtedly, the money wasted on payoffs, useless projects, redundant contracts, no-show jobs, and rigged bidding was astronomical. Not to mention the honest vendors, developers, and visionaries who simply walked away when they learned that doing business in the area meant having to violate the law and their own principles.

The county case became the largest corruption investigation in Ohio history. Dimora was convicted of thirty-two charges including bribery, racketeering, conspiracy, and tax violations. The man who refused to leave office earned the distinction of receiving the longest federal prison sentence for any sitting public official—twenty-eight years. Inmate number 56275-060 at Federal Correctional Institution, Elkton, Ohio, gave up fine dining for baloney sandwiches and Flamin' Hot Cheetos from the prison commissary. Taxpayers are still picking up his tab. But the people of Cuyahoga County clearly got the message: times had changed.

One year after the raids, county voters elected to change their form of government so that, hopefully, an abuse of power of this magnitude would not happen again. A single elected county executive now leads an eleven-member county council with members representing distinct districts. Those council members serve as a check on the power of the county executive. The old countywide elected offices filled by cousins, aunts, and no-shows became appointed positions staffed by professionals, instead of politicians. County residents had placed their faith in the Bureau's credibility. Now they were taking the first steps to restoring faith in their own government. In the decade since Dimora went to prison, the Cleveland area's economy and culture experienced a resurgence for a variety of reasons. The region's rapid urban renewal put it in the forefront of national media attention covering its revival. I believe the men and women of the FBI had something to do with that.

The FBI in Cleveland, as in cities around America, helped restore credibility to city and county government. This couldn't have happened unless the FBI itself was perceived as having enough credibility to get the job done. In this best possible scenario, the people of Cuyahoga County were empowered to take matters into their own hands and put changes in place to help maintain their belief in their elected leaders. That's the power of credibility.

Ask yourself whether you have cultivated the kind of credibility that allows your team to trust you as the promoter and preserver of the group's values. If you think the answer is yes, that's great. But understand that credibility needs regular care and maintenance. If you lack credibility, people are less likely to accept the values you or your organization want to embody. Employees, teammates, or voters who don't view you as a legitimate representative of collective values will abandon either you, those values, or both. You don't need to be perfect to be credible, just passionate about getting it right.

7

CONSISTENCY

P REACHING TO THE CHOIR IS A PIECE OF CAKE COM-
pared to converting the agnostic. Likewise, it's much easier to consistently champion your standards if everyone around
you agrees with them. But the real world is seldom so tranquil.
Individuals, universities, businesses, and yes, even churches
get into deep quagmires when, under stress, they abandon their
principles when it becomes too painful to defend them. Stories
abound of colleges covering up misconduct by star athletes,
companies ignoring sexual harassment allegations against top
executives, and government agencies burying news that makes
them look bad. Inevitably, though, the cost of compromising
your standards turns out to be greater than the discomfort of
adhering to them.

Like the FBI, organizations can enhance their capacity to

consistently do the right thing under pressure by empowering employees to speak out, elevating leaders who embody core values, and instinctively defending against threats to those values. Steady preservation of values offers the added benefit of resilience in the face of adversity because it allows you to pivot and adapt as needed without jettisoning what you stand for. During the COVID-19 pandemic of 2020, we saw some of our nation's leaders abandon proven crisis management precepts, and even American values, in favor of shorter-term gratification and political and economic expediency. Other leaders, primarily state governors, stuck with core crisis concepts and values like preservation of life, data-driven decisions, and transparent truth-telling despite intense pressure to reopen their states and ease public health restrictions. Consistency saved lives.

The Bureau, during my tenure, was particularly consistent at adhering to its core values under stress even when defending those values meant risking the wrath of our partners in the military, the CIA, and even the White House. Following the terror attacks of September 11, 2001, I was reassigned from leading the Miami Division's white-collar and corruption squads to heading a newly formed Joint Terrorism Task Force for South Florida. The Miami office, along with the entire FBI, became part of a massive strategic shift. The FBI needed to transform from an agency that was great at investigating an incident after it happened to an agency that could predict and prevent what was about to occur. From the tragedy of 9/11 to the deadly anthrax attacks just one month later, unprecedented events were unfolding while the U.S. intelligence community, military, and law enforcement struggled with how to respond. During crises, or under the strain of tumultuous change, families, corporations, and even governments often lose their bearing and their moral compass. Tumult was a constant component of FBI life but perhaps never more so than in the weeks and months following 9/11.

In the 9/11 aftermath, FBI Headquarters tapped the Miami office, which covered Latin America, to coordinate the growing Bureau presence at Guantánamo Bay (GTMO), Cuba. The FBI was a key agency responsible for gleaning intelligence from detainee interviews on any plans for additional attacks against America. FBI special agents and intelligence analysts needed to be physically present at GTMO because any time lapse between a detainee's disclosing a new homeland attack, sleeper cell, or target and the processing of that intel by CIA or military interrogators was unacceptable. Further, while the administration was wrestling with the issue of military tribunals, the FBI was charged with preparing for the possibility of federal criminal charges against detainees and others. That meant someone might have to assemble prosecutions and testify in court back home. Clandestine CIA officers and covert military intelligence collectors were neither trained nor willing to do that, for fear of compromising their identities.

FBI agents and intelligence analysts started taking the quick government flight from Miami to GTMO and setting up shop with their counterparts from across the intelligence community. But as the agents observed detainee interrogations, they witnessed conduct they had to report—to me. One afternoon, the supervisor of Miami's al-Qaeda squad walked into my office with two of his best agents, just back from GTMO, and closed the door. The supervisor asked the agents to describe to me what was happening just ninety miles south of us. The agents advised that they had walked out of interrogations by military and civilian interrogators at GTMO rather than become witnesses to what might become excessive force and civil rights allegations and violations. The Miami-based agents explained that the interrogators were guided in part by the U.S. Army Field Manual on Interrogation. They handed me a copy of the manual and asked me to read portions of it. Clearly, we had a problem.

Any intelligence extracted using the manual's more hands-on or physical techniques described by the agents could be deemed coerced and therefore worthless in U.S. federal court. Moreover, additional methods like prolonged exposure to temperature extremes, food and water deprivation, and gross offenses to Islamic religious customs placed detainees under enough duress that they might fabricate stories simply to get some relief. The agents sitting in my office were tough, bright, and experienced terrorism specialists; there were no wimps among them.

The agents' mission was to elicit reliable intelligence and prepare solid cases for trial in federal court. To achieve this, they had to play by FBI and Department of Justice rules. I was proud of those agents and humbled by the trust they placed in me. I told the squad supervisor to draft a communication to FBIHQ with all the details and concerns. I handed the memo to the SAC of the Miami Division, who approved the communication to Director Mueller without blinking an eye.

That communication helped prompt an internal investigation by the FBI's Inspection Division. The FBI needed to know if any FBI employees had witnessed or participated in violations of FBI standards, or worse. The extensive inquiry found that none of the witnessed acts of abuse had been carried out by an FBI employee. The Bureau's own investigation was over, but a much larger question was looming concerning the consistent application of values and methods across American agencies and organizations.

The FBI's inquiry contributed to the fiery debate in Washington over military versus civilian trials for hostile combatants, and over which agency should take the lead in terrorist interrogations. A convincing case was made to Congress and the George W. Bush administration that they couldn't have it both ways. They couldn't have the military and CIA use their own rules to interrogate subjects and then try to bring those subjects into the criminal justice system where entirely different rules applied. They couldn't claim violent extremists were the antithesis of what America stood for and then endorse behavior by our own citizens that undermined that argument. Ultimately, President Bush ordered creation of an interagency High-Value Interrogation Group led by the FBI. The Bureau's position may not have been popular, but it was consistent with its core values, standards, and mission. More important, the Bureau's stance upheld American values.

I've been to GTMO. I've seen the hostile combatants in cages, pacing back and forth, reading their U.S. government–supplied Korans, praying five times daily. I've watched men, some who wanted nothing more than to kill the first American they could grab, play soccer on a makeshift field of sand and gravel while U.S. military guards stood watch. I've observed those same prisoners hoard their new favorite breakfast of cinnamon-raisin bagels and cream cheese packets like coveted currency. Seeing violent Islamic radicals (as many, though not all, of the detainees were) becoming fond of a typically Jewish American food and playing soccer like kids in a schoolyard reinforced for me the notion that the FBI's proven and consistent approach to interrogating people would work with these people, too.

GTMO was the first time the FBI had ever played a protracted role at a military detention camp. Institutions and individuals can be shaken to their core by what I call the "strain of the strange." When threatened by an unprecedented challenge of overwhelming proportions, the fight-or-flight response can cause people to not only flee the scene but to abandon well-established principles. All too often, severe stress associated with the unforeseen, or the never before seen, serves as a false rationale to jettison everything that has previously worked, at the precise time when proven practices are needed the most.

We seem to think that if what we're facing is radically inconsistent from anything we've ever seen, then some radically inconsistent approach must be required to resolve it. This logic is flawed whether we're talking about a nation dealing with a global pandemic or we're running a domestic security agency where the bizarre is a weekly occurrence.

THE UNCOMMON AND THE STRANGE MADE FREQUENT APpearances at GTMO. The challenge was to discern whether what we were seeing was consistent with the Bureau's mission and values. Sometimes this challenge was gravely serious; other times, not so much. One afternoon, when FBI Miami was still overseeing Bureau operations at GTMO, my boss called me to his office. He had plans for my weekend. Something was developing that sounded inconsistent with the FBI's role.

The boss had gotten a call from the GTMO military commander, who was profusely grateful that one of our agents had arranged for the chart-topping Grammy-award-winning band Hootie & the Blowfish to play an upcoming gig for the troops at U.S. Naval Station Guantánamo Bay. Of course, we had absolutely no idea what he was talking about. As it turned out, a Miami agent had a connection to the band from Columbia, South Carolina. They had offered to play, free of charge, in appreciation for the servicemen and -women, and the military had arranged a transport plane to take them, their crew, and all their equipment to the base. Since the Bureau was all about consistency, and since putting on a rock concert was just a tad inconsistent with the FBI's mission, someone had to get a handle on what was happening. That would be me, along with FBI Miami's chief legal counsel.

We booked ourselves on the next government flight to GTMO and packed our bags for the weekend. Once we arrived, we liked what we saw. The veteran agent who arranged the concert had been working at GTMO for a while. He was one of those back-slapping guys who knew how to make friends and influence people. He understood the FBI's role on base was delicate, and he was trying his best to win over the top brass there. He just forgot to tell his own bosses what he was up to. It turned out that arranging entertainment for the troops was consistent with how strongly the Bureau values its liaison with essential partners. Sometimes taking a broader view of your mission can help preserve your values.

GTMO was a large base with both a civilian and a military population. Some of the troops assigned there were permitted to move their families into base housing. There were two schools, a church, fast-food joints, and military-run shops. There was also a seldom-used open-air stadium. The night of the concert, everything on base stopped; even church events were canceled. If you were on base, you were at the stadium—kids, spouses, troops, everyone. The agent who coordinated all this was brought up onstage and introduced to the whole base as the FBI guy who made it happen. Cheers went up. It was a masterful liaison move. Oh, and it turned out, lead singer Darius Rucker and his buddies were very cool dudes. They really cared about the troops. Just don't call Darius "Hootie," by the way; he doesn't like it.

EVEN THOUGH THE BUREAU REGULARLY RESOLVED EXOTIC and unparalleled threats, murder by anthrax was a new one for all of us. The Miami office was just coming up for air less than a month after the 9/11 attacks. As I made my move from our downstairs ops center to my upstairs office, I welcomed the chance to take a breath and close out my tenure as the head of Miami's White-Collar Crime Branch. The boss had asked me to take over a new counterterrorism program and expanded Joint Terrorism Task Force. First, I had to clean out my remaining white-collar duties. I began to wade into an in-box bursting with overdue requests for case extensions, investigative technique approvals, and other typically routine management decisions in one of the most productive white-collar programs in the FBI. The siren call of comfort and normalcy was beckoning that first week in October. Well, at least it was until the phone on my desk rang. I could see the call had been transferred by the SAC's administrative assistant. Inconsistency was about to visit again.

Just a few weeks prior, I had attended executive training at Quantico. Over the years, I was impressed by the caliber of the FBI's training. I could point to courses and instructors that developed me as an investigator and a manager. My only two issues involved the Bureau's approach to management training. First, back then, there were precious few instructors or speakers from outside the FBI. I understood the need to ensure that we learned the Bureau's way of seeing things and to mitigate the risk of exposing outsiders to sensitive matters, but this insularity sometimes created a kind of echo chamber of FBI thought within the classrooms. Second, particularly with leadership training, it was often "too little, too late." By the time I could get a slot in a certain course, I was already serving in the role the course was designed for. That meant I sometimes had already learned the hard way what was being taught in the course.

Thankfully, that wasn't true for the Quantico course I attended just before answering that call transferred to my desk the first week of October 2001. The course had ended with a major tabletop exercise of a full-blown FBI response to a biochemical attack. Because of an upward trend in hoax "white powder" mailings, the exercise planners decided the bacteria of choice for this drill would be anthrax. When I got back to Miami, the boss asked how the training went. I half kiddingly told him that if we ever faced an anthrax attack, "I'm your guy." Me and my big mouth.

Starting soon after 9/11, someone or some group began mailing letters filled with anthrax spores to multiple major media outlets including ABC News, CBS News, NBC News, and the *New York Post*, and later to U.S. senators Patrick Leahy and Tom Daschle. Thankfully, no one had been killed. Yet.

I punched the flashing extension button on my desk phone,

lifted the receiver to my ear, and found myself talking to a physician who served as the Palm Beach County medical director. She introduced herself and quickly got to the point. She said there was a patient at JFK Medical Center who was rapidly dying of what looked like anthrax poisoning. She had convened a meeting in her conference room and needed the FBI there. When she asked how fast I could get to her office, I told her I'd make it from North Miami Beach to West Palm Beach in forty minutes. It was a sixty-mile drive. If that calculation seems ambitious to you, you'd be right.

As I jumped into my bucar, I let the SAC know what was happening and called the unit chief at Quantico who had helped design the anthrax exercise. I told him where I was headed and why, and he pledged to have the Bureau PhD microbiologists, whom I had met during the training, standing by to assess whatever I learned from the medical director. There's no way my fellow motorists on I-95 north would ever have guessed that the guy in the black supercharged V6 Pontiac Bonneville SSEi rocketing past them with blue strobes and siren was responding to a suspected anthrax poisoning.

I nailed my promised arrival time in West Palm. I abandoned my car outside the county medical office and took long, purposeful strides into the building, through the corridor, and finally into the conference room. As I knocked and swung open the door, a group of somber-faced health professionals seated around a small table turned and stared. To me, the look on those faces was a combination of gravity and despair. "I'm

Frank Figliuzzi, FBI." The medical director didn't bother with introductions, she simply advised that staff from JFK Medical Center were on the open phone line and instructed them to start briefing.

I quickly learned that a sixty-three-year-old male was brought into the emergency room by his wife at 2:15 A.M. on October 2 and fell into a coma one hour later. It was initially believed he might have meningitis, but treatment for that and other ailments had failed. The man was in a coma and dying the kind of violently unpleasant death that medical textbooks associate with anthrax. It was those symptoms combined with an all-important blood sample that prompted the possibility of inhalational anthrax poisoning. The doctors knew that if they were right about the match between the images under their microscopes and the images in their diagnostic manuals, this could be much bigger than anyone had dealt with before. As the voices on the other end of the conference call began to describe the unusual rod-shaped, purple-stained bacteria, I called time-out. I wanted the local scientists talking to FBI scientists, not to an English literature major with a law degree.

The PhDs at Quantico had already texted me asking for a detailed visual description of what the technicians were seeing under their microscopes. I told the room I was now connecting to the FBI's experts so they could listen in real time. I put my BlackBerry on speakerphone so our two scientists could hopefully hear the folks on the hospital line describing the appearance of whatever was in the patient's blood. I was concerned about the clarity of the connection, but in the middle of the briefing, I received a simple text from the Bureau's doctors: "They are describing anthrax." So much for a return to comfort and normalcy.

Robert Stevens, a British-born, sixty-three-year-old photo editor for the *Sun* weekly tabloid, worked at the American Media Incorporated (AMI) building in Boca Raton. After a visit to North Carolina, he began having flulike symptoms. His wife brought him to the emergency room suffering from shortness of breath, and he was admitted to the hospital. Stevens fell into a coma one hour later and was officially diagnosed with anthrax poisoning on October 4. This diagnosis, confirmed by the Centers for Disease Control and Prevention in Atlanta, launched an all-out investigative blitz to determine exactly where Stevens had inhaled anthrax.

Ordinarily, a patient presenting with anthrax symptoms might not generate a call to the FBI. *Bacillus anthracis*, as scientists call it, is a bacterium found in nature. Anthrax spreads through contact with its spores, which often exist in hooved animals like cattle, camels, sheep, and goats. In fact, in some parts of the world, anthrax is called "wool handler's disease" because people who work in the early phases of wool processing are often exposed to small, less than lethal doses. In the United States, anthrax is sometimes rampant in the white-tailed deer population in South Texas. The spores can enter your body through broken skin, through inhaling, or even by eating an infected animal. The bacterium is commonly found in Africa,

Asia, and southern Europe. But there was nothing common about this case. Doctors had already questioned Stevens's wife to identify what epidemiologists call the "vector" by which her husband might have contracted anthrax. Their quest for a vector consistent with anthrax came up empty.

Was he a hunter? No.

Did he spend a lot of time in forests? No, he went for brief walks to take photos.

Did he recently travel to Africa, Asia, or southern Europe? No.

Did he work with or purchase animal skins, furs, or rugs? No.

Was he exposed to deer or other animals? No.

A visit to the Stevens's residence found no obvious culprit. We were less than a month from the mass carnage of the 9/11 terror attacks, and we had no natural explanation for why Robert Stevens was dying from anthrax. We knew someone had been targeting news organizations, sending them anthrax-filled letters. Although few people would consider the AMI tabloids like the *Sun* or the *National Enquirer* to be serious media publications, those papers were part of the media industry, and Stevens worked there.

The county medical director was a no-nonsense, take-charge kind of person; she might have made a great FBI agent. She made it clear, and I agreed, that the AMI building needed to be evacuated and quarantined. We quickly ran through our legal options to empty the building and keep it that way. I offered that the building was potentially a crime scene, and the FBI could deploy agents to "hold" the building and start drafting a search warrant to be signed by a judge. I noted we could also get the consent of the owner to simply close the building, yet that wouldn't give us the legal authority to keep the building off-limits. It was quickly apparent that the doctor possessed the fastest and purest power to clear and close AMI headquarters: "I'm closing the building for public health reasons effective immediately," she said. I told the good doctor that I had agents standing by in the AMI parking lot ready to join her staff in posting official signs on the entrances. She agreed.

I placed the FBI Miami Evidence Response Team (ERT) on standby and arrived at AMI right around the end of business hours. A handful of agents were waiting as I pulled into the mostly empty parking lot. We posted the Health Department notices but couldn't ignore the fact that some of the cars in the lot didn't belong to us; that meant there might still be people in the building. The FBI experts at Quantico had emphatically instructed us not to enter the building without HAZMAT gear. After unsuccessfully trying to call the AMI main switchboard, we decided to contact AMI executives to determine if anyone was still in the building. AMI leadership was out of town, and they advised us that they had no way of definitively knowing which employees might still be at work. We ran some of the license plates on cars still in the parking lot and got some names but couldn't confirm any cell-phone numbers belonging to those names.

One ERT agent, never much of a rule follower, announced he was going in to evacuate people. If we waited for full HAZMAT gear and decontamination equipment to arrive, someone in that building could stumble upon whatever was killing Stevens, and that would be on us. I gave the agent the official line that I would not approve what he was suggesting and that it was unsafe. He said he completely understood, then while I was on the phone with HQ, he went in anyway. There were indeed a few people left in that building, and although they were totally clueless as to what was happening, they were lucky to be alive. So was our agent. But Robert Stevens wasn't so lucky. On October 5, 2001, he became the first of five people to die in a series of anthrax attacks.

It was well past time for me to have an in-person talk with the chief of police for Boca Raton. This was happening in his city and we would need his support in a big way if we were going to pull off the first-ever HAZMAT murder crime scene search in FBI history. The world's media was about to descend upon this beach resort city, and we would need perimeter security, joint press release coordination, and all-around partnership. Besides that, the mayor and city council would soon start demanding answers from their chief. The chief was an experienced professional and a graduate of the FBI National Academy. The Bureau already enjoyed a good working relationship with his department. We had some task force office space in town and regularly worked with Boca PD detectives on drug and organized crime cases. When I finished briefing the chief on what was happening, his face took on the look of someone trying to figure out whether they were being pranked. After a brief pause, the chief stated, "Whatever you need, just keep me briefed." There would be plenty to brief.

Anthrax would later kill two postal workers and a hospital employee in New York, as well as an elderly woman in Connecticut. Seventeen other people fell ill during these attacks. As it often does for large-scale, multiple field office investigations, the FBI consolidated all the anthrax incidents under one investigation and assigned it a case name: Amerithrax. I became the on-scene commander for the evidence recovery effort at the first anthrax murder scene in U.S. history. Well, technically I was the FBI's on-scene commander. An epidemiologist who flew in from the Centers for Disease Control and Prevention (CDC) in Atlanta seemed to have his own take on things.

The FBI and the CDC were both in the mystery-solving business. The Bureau knew how to work complex crime scenes and terrorism investigations. And the CDC's physician epidemiologists were pros at tracking and containing a deadly illness outbreak. You would think our respective skills and experiences would produce a marriage made in heaven. Except this was a mail-order shotgun marriage between complete strangers speaking entirely different languages. Consistency in mission didn't equate to compatibility during a crisis.

FBI agents come to work every day alongside task force partners from dozens of local, state, and federal law enforcement agencies, all under one roof. We often deputize our police partners as federal officers and give them the same security clearances as us. We generally share a common language and understand, even with glitches, that information-sharing and cooperation are the only ways to accomplish our collective mission. But the anthrax challenge was not a cop-to-cop thing. It was an unprecedented crisis that shoved together two government agencies quite accustomed to their respective roles as the five-hundred-pound gorillas of their own domains—public health and law enforcement. In this case, those symbolic alpha primates were embodied in a CDC doctor from Atlanta and me. Our honeymoon was not exactly marital bliss.

Our tiny eight-by-six-foot makeshift command post trailer in the middle of AMI's asphalt parking lot was more of a cage than a honeymoon suite. It took a couple of days before the CDC dispatched my Atlanta counterpart to colocate with me. By then, the FBI Miami ERT, now joined by CDC operators, were moving methodically in HAZMAT gear through the AMI building, collecting microscopic samples to trace the route of the deadly spores, and shipping off those samples for rapid testing at the approved Florida laboratory. We were now getting near real-time lab results, which while not guaranteed, were damn good indicators of where we were or were not finding anthrax inside the building. Then the CDC doctor showed up.

I'm a big believer in colocating leaders during a crisis or joint operation. Despite all the high-tech, state-of-the-art teleconferencing and video capabilities, there is nothing like sitting elbow to elbow, sharing and responding to intelligence as it develops, brainstorming what-ifs, and agreeing on what and when to brief to the media and to respective chains of command. Putting decision makers in one place has another, less intangible benefit. During any precious downtime, sitting together allows you to learn what you might have in common with your newfound friend. That is, unless one of you doesn't want to play nicely in the sandbox.

The lead CDC doctor was initially ensconced up in the administrative command center at the FBI's West Palm Beach Resident Agency. Our SAC and other FBI managers and case agents were housed there. This was where extremely detailed regular written briefings were drafted for headquarters bosses, investigative leads were assigned and tracked, joint press releases were crafted, and endless inquiries were fielded from top brass at FBI Washington and CDC Atlanta. But the minute-by-minute tactical work and decision-making was happening outside the AMI building and inside our trailer. Even more important, we established a direct line with the laboratory to receive our sampling results and decide which twist or turn to make next within the building. We immediately and often simultaneously shared these results with the CDC doctor, but his perception that the FBI might know things before he did drove him bananas.

The CDC doc insisted that all lab results go to him first. He began yelling and hanging up during our phone calls. I told him we could easily remedy his perception that results were being hidden or delayed if he simply left the comfortable confines of FBI West Palm Beach and joined me in my lovely trailer. I was wrong about that.

Soon after the doc took a seat beside me, he pronounced something to the effect that this was a public health crisis, public health always came first, and therefore, he was in charge. I was dumbfounded that at this point in the game anyone would be caught up with being in charge. I tried explaining what he already knew: we were jointly working an active crime scene with both FBI and CDC HAZMAT operators; the nasal passages of all AMI employees had already been swabbed and tested for anthrax; lab results of samples from inside the building were strongly pointing to the mail room; and anthrax mailings around the country made it likely that we were under yet another terror attack. I told the doctor this was a joint public health and law enforcement crisis and we were going to proceed as such. The doc responded by again asserting that he needed to see and interpret all lab results first, and that all communication with the regional and Florida state labs would be through him. I called BS. Then I called FBI Headquarters.

FBIHQ was incredulous. Are you certain what you're telling us about this guy is accurate? "Yes, I have witnesses. You can also just ask him yourself. He'll be happy to tell you that he's in charge." HQ called CDC headquarters and relayed the concern that their guy might not be the man for the job. CDC, equally incredulous, interviewed their doc. He was gone the next day. The CDC immediately deployed Dr. Richard Besser to join me in the parking lot. I could not have imagined a better partner than Besser. We shared the mutual goal of getting the job done through complete transparency. Dr. Besser is a class act who later went on to become the acting director of the CDC, an ABC News chief health and medical editor, and the president and CEO of the Robert Wood Johnson Foundation. The fact that he was dealing with an unprecedented situation didn't cause Besser to abandon his professionalism, it caused him to cling to it. He understood the concept of consistency in a crisis.

The members of the FBI Miami ERT were the unsung heroes of the anthrax crisis. Here's why. We had a decision to make as soon as we realized that we were dealing with an anthrax-filled, three-story, sixty-thousand-square-foot building linked to the horrific death of a man who simply decided to show up for work on the wrong day. The team could wait for the folks at Quantico who specialize in HAZMAT evidence collection or they could suit up and go in now. The Quantico teams were already thinly stretched responding to anthrax mailings at the U.S. Capitol and in New York City. If we requested, those experts could get here when they could, or they could provide initial guidance and direction over the phone to our capable team. I looked the Miami team leader in the eye and asked him if our team was up to the task. This agent, a former navy officer and forensic dental odontologist prior to joining the FBI, was never one to turn down a challenge. He knew his team could do it.

Despite what might be portrayed on various TV shows, FBI ERT members volunteer from the agent and professional support employee ranks. They don't do this full-time and they aren't picked for this right out of college. They all have caseloads or other assignments of their own. Even though they are plenty busy working their assigned investigations and primary duties, they raise their hands to receive highly specialized training on evidence collection in extremely diverse and challenging environments. Often their work is routine, such as when they dust for latent fingerprints, test for gunpowder residue on a suspect's hands, or vacuum up hairs and fibers that might later be tied to a bad guy. All too often, ERTs are deployed to gruesome murder or shooting scenes, or even to conduct archaeological digs at sites where bodies are believed to have been buried. Back in 2001, these teams were just starting to become adept at gathering evidence within hazardous and even deadly environments.

Many of the Miami team members had just recently received HAZMAT training, where they learned how to suit up in those white, Level C suits, breathe through powered air-purifying respirators (PAPRs), and go through a decontamination ritual after each high-risk entry. Those folks likely thought that their training would be put to the test during entries into clandestine meth labs, but none of them could have predicted they would soon be operating inside a fatal anthrax environment. Moreover, none of those team members would have guessed this kind of deployment would come just a few weeks after their marathon of multiple entries into the South Florida homes of the 9/11 terrorists. For them, crisis had become a constant.

For about a week, FBI Miami personnel floated like white-robed ghosts in and out of the AMI building. They methodically swabbed corridors, walls, desks, and even the ceilings. Each team entry was strictly timed to avoid overtaxing not only the breathing apparatus but also the human wearing it. South Florida heat and humidity can be oppressive, but things get downright scary when you wrap someone head to toe in a synthetic Tyvek suit with elastic wristbands, then duct-tape that polyethylene outfit around their wrists, ankles, and face, all while making them breathe through a mask. Then march those same people into a three-story building with limited air circulation. Each team leader received regular radio transmissions reminding them of the time remaining before they had to pull their team out to safety. Yet the process was only half over once the team stepped out of AMI.

As the members exited the building, they queued up for the decontamination wash process, capably run by the Boca Raton Fire Department. As hoses flushed water over each team member, masks and hoods were peeled off and suits were shed like discarded cocoons. The faces of the fatigued teams were as white as their protective garb, and perspiration streamed like a waterfall into the decon troughs where members stood, sometimes swaying on the verge of collapse. And there were still more health and safety protocols.

Medics took and charted each team member's blood pressure and passed any concerns on to the FBI doctor on-scene. And as if their body functions weren't taxed enough, most of the teams agreed to go on the recommended regimen of thirty to sixty days of an antibiotic to counter anthrax exposure. The drug wreaked havoc on their gastrointestinal systems and had the extra bonus of extreme phototoxicity. That meant many were walking around with flash burns from the slightest sun exposure. The prescribed medication was the gift that kept on giving things that nobody needed or wanted. The effects of consistent stress were becoming visible.

The anthrax operation was understandably stressful. There are different kinds of stress in life, and it's important to recognize the differences. For example, there's the stress that's self-induced and there's the stress that's thrown at us from others. Neither of those are particularly healthy, but we can learn to deal with them smartly and even negate them. Most FBI agents will tell you that there are also two other kinds of stress—real stress and artificial stress. For law enforcement and intelligence professionals, real stress is when someone's life is on the line, maybe even your own. Perhaps you're racing to locate a kidnapped child, chasing a fugitive down a dark alley, sneaking into a gang leader's house to plant a court-authorized microphone, or making decisions that might prevent the next anthrax attack. That's real stress.

Then there's the artificial kind of stress. That kind of stress usually involves people in dark suits, sometimes with fancy titles, often on the phone, and frequently, many miles away. They demand information, reports, briefings, forms, and answers at the very moment when those are the last things you should be spending time on. It's not really their fault, because there are other people in more expensive suits, with even fancier titles, who are demanding those same things from them. I consistently experienced artificial stress in the anthrax case. I just had to put it all in perspective, and my time spent at FBIHQ helped me to do that.

The FBI is wise to make its leaders take assignments at FBIHQ. During those postings, we come to understand and appreciate that we are part of a much bigger picture, and that whatever we're working on in the field is just one piece of a greater puzzle—a puzzle that needs to get solved. That was particularly true during the nationwide anthrax investigation. Hence the endless phone calls at all hours of the day and night. Again, as was true with 9/11, sleep eluded me; it was a sure sign of the impact of consistent stress.

Fortunately, the Miami office knew the artificial stress was coming. The boss set up an entire team, including supervisory levels, that did nothing but prepare multiple written and verbal briefings for FBIHQ throughout the day, every single day. How many entries did the ERT make today? How many samples were taken? Where were the highest concentrations of anthrax spores? Have you sampled the local and regional post offices for anthrax yet? What were those results? How many investigative interviews were done of AMI employees, family members, postal workers, trash collectors, friends, enemies, and so on? When is your next press briefing and what will you say? Why is Governor Jeb Bush asking for a briefing? When will you give it to him? The West Palm Beach Resident Agency (RA) was the base for this administrative operation. For the most part, this kind of separation of duties kept me free to run the evidence collection effort in Boca. For the most part. Unless, say, perhaps the White House had a question for me. And they did.

As I stepped into the trailer very early one morning, an agent holding the hard-line phone told me that FBIHQ needed to speak to me right now. I asked the agent if he knew who was on the line. He repeated a name that I knew belonged to a senior executive from the Counterterrorism Division, then added, "He says he has someone from the White House who needs to ask you some questions about our scientific approach to the collection." Another agent, correctly reading my half-awake face, quickly handed me a cup of coffee. There were now three of us staring at the blinking phone line. The Bureau is a chain of command organization. There were several management tiers separating me from the official on the other end of that phone. People with fancy suits and fancier titles generally don't directly speak to the guy in the trailer, especially not at 6:00 A.M., and especially not with the White House on the line. Then again, we had never had an anthrax attack before.

I asked if the ERT leader was on-scene yet. He knew every inch of the inside of the AMI building and every facet of our collection techniques. I was told he was still in bed getting some much-needed sleep. I decided that his rest was far more important to our success that day than whatever question was going to be asked by Washington. Besides, I had taken great pains to understand precisely what we were doing in that building, how we were doing it, and why our approach was the best. Before approving our collection plans, I fired endless questions at the FBI microbiologists, CDC epidemiologists, state laboratory scientists, and our own evidence technicians. I owned the decisions we were making in that building, right or wrong. I took the phone receiver from the agent.

Clearly, the HQ bigwig on the line already had plenty of morning coffee, as evidenced by his high-speed, high-volume delivery. "Figliuzzi, I have the White House science adviser on hold. She's going to ask you some detailed questions about the sampling technique you are using." His voice was now at an even higher decibel. "Are you going to be able to answer her questions or not?" As calmly as possible I responded, "I haven't heard the questions yet, but this is my crime scene. If I can't answer her questions, then no one else can." That seemed to calm him down. He patched through the White House scientist. As soon as she began her question, I knew she was wrestling with the same technical issue over sampling alternatives that we had already resolved. I told her which option we had chosen, she pronounced it correct and ended the call. By now a small crowd had packed into our humble abode, and all of us breathed a sigh of relief. Artificial stress resolved, at least for now.

I could see the fatigue setting in on weary bodies and faces. The same bodies that had just lived through our 9/11 investigation in South Florida were now on the front line of a different but equally unfathomable crisis. Several times each day at the AMI site, I would make rounds through the parking lot for the express purpose of checking on the morale and well-being of our team at each of the various stations we had set up. There was the evidence logging and storage station, the decontamination station, the microbiologist command bus, the ERT trailer, a communications post, a medical station, and more. We had two daily all-hands briefings to discuss the day's objectives and accomplishments, but my rounds allowed folks to ask me questions, express concerns, and float rumors in a more personal setting. Consistently taking the pulse of your people during a protracted crisis isn't a luxury, it's a necessity.

Many on our team talked openly about concerns at home with worried family members, and kids asking if that was their dad or mom they saw in the white suit on TV. There were a lot of questions from both males and females about the long-term effects of extended antibiotic doses, and even whether Cipro (ciprofloxacin) or doxycycline was the correct drug of choice. This was not established science. I referred most of those questions to our FBI doctor who traveled down from D.C., while letting my team know that they weren't going through this alone—I, too, was taking Cipro. I don't know for sure, but maybe knowing that a manager was asking similar questions helped a little. I hope so. My walk-arounds provided both the team members and me some momentary stress relief. There was also some comic relief.

The AMI search site was an intensely serious scene. Yet anyone who regularly deals with gravely serious matters of life, death, or national security will tell you they can find humor in the strangest places. Cops, ER nurses, paramedics, and doctors all have stories to tell that still bring a smile years later. FBI agents are no exception. For example, we talked with AMI CEO David Pecker and his staff in order to keep them briefed on the status of their building, obtain keys and blueprints, and ask questions about the HVAC system. We made Pecker an offer, realizing that after we were done, the entire building might forever be off-limits, or at least until AMI could find someone to decontaminate it. He accepted our offer.

On a phone call one day, our team leader told Pecker that if he could identify one or two of his most valuable possessions and describe where in his office they were, we would try to remove and decontaminate them. It didn't take the CEO long to tell us that hanging outside his office were two large framed photographs. What he most wanted from his office were a photo of Elvis's corpse lying in a coffin and a fabricated photo of a half-human, half-bat creature known as Bat Boy. I was sorry we asked.

There was another aspect of our search operation that I found amusing, because the only other alternative would have been to let it drive me crazy. Since we were making history as America's first anthrax murder scene, FBIHQ wanted to document every move and decision I made. I got a call one day advising that a "scribe" would be arriving from Washington for the sole purpose of shadowing me and memorializing everything I did. The well-meaning young man who showed up profusely apologized and assured me he was not a spy from HQ. He documented my daily rhythm of briefings, planning, and execution and noted any significant decisions and interaction with the CDC and laboratories. More than once I suggested he might want to note my choice of lunch and average time in the porta potty. He disappeared after a couple of days.

While working on this book, I checked out the open source accounts of the anthrax death of Robert Stevens. A lot of them were flat-out wrong. Here's what happened as best as we could determine. Our search established a strong trail of anthrax spores from the point where the U.S. mail entered the AMI building, into the mail room, and from the mail room through the building on the path the mail cart took, and particularly to two locations. Any time mail arrived that wasn't addressed to a specific individual, perhaps just to "The National Enquirer," it was tossed into a designated bin perched atop a shelf in the mail room. Sealed and silent, such "general address" parcels patiently awaited the next stop on their respective journeys. Their courses were charted by a young female staffer who opened each missive, assessed its message, and forwarded it, via the office mail cart, to the most logical recipient.

But one such letter wasn't so patient. Though silent, it was already delivering a murderous message. Mingled amid the other mail, an envelope was leaking microscopic spores that coated the other parcels, spilled through holes in the base of the bin, and showered onto the shelf below. The invisible cascade pooled on the surface of an open ream of copy paper stored just beneath the bin. Robert Stevens had some copying to do and he needed that paper. Based on investigative interviews and laboratory findings, I was convinced Stevens grabbed that stack of paper and headed to a copy machine. That would be the very machine our team found covered with anthrax, not just on the copier, but on the floor below it, the area around it, and even on the ceiling above it. Stevens, age sixty-two and already compromised by a respiratory ailment, likely inserted the ream, stood over the copier, pressed a button, and inhaled a high-speed stream of death.

Our theory was bolstered by the spore trail that started at the mail room and stopped at the desk of a young woman in her twenties. Her duties included opening the general mail and figuring out who should deal with it. But where was she? Her name wasn't among the long list of employees we had already interviewed and swabbed for nasal testing. Initial attempts to reach her by phone hadn't worked. The lead investigator and I exchanged a glance. Without saying a word, we knew what each of us was thinking. Was the woman who opened this package lying dead or incapacitated somewhere? My next instructions were obvious: "Find her. Keep calling her, go to her home, find her parents, find her relatives, just find her."

When I've found myself dropped into a large-scale crisis or gravely serious operation, it has been sometimes helpful, grounding, and even mildly amusing, to be reminded that all around me, people are going on with their lives, sometimes oblivious to whatever grave scenario is playing out just under their nose. That's a good thing. In fact, that's why we have an FBI, so everyone else can go about their business without the weight of the world on their shoulders. As I drove each day to our anthrax site, I passed kids getting on school buses, moms and dads headed to work, and joggers running their routes. Boca is a resort town, so there were even people on vacation. Even AMI mail clerks take vacations. And, of course, that's exactly what Stephanie Daily was doing—enjoying some time off.

Our team finally reached her by phone. "May I ask how you're feeling?" Stephanie felt fine. An agent asked her if she could talk in person. "Sure," she said. Once the team sat her down, she was a wealth of information. We still had not found our package, but we had photos of the envelopes delivered to other news organizations and to Congress. Our investigators showed these images to the smiling, upbeat young lady and asked her if she remembered opening anything similar, perhaps containing white powder. She did indeed. In fact, she remembered it well.

The white powder spilling all over her desk particularly annoyed Stephanie. She bundled up the envelope and its contents, tossed it in the trash, and marched off to the restroom for some paper towels. Next, she scrubbed her hands with soap and warm water, then made her way back to her desk to wipe it down until all the white powder was gone. Once her cleanup was done, she chucked the used paper towels into her trash can. This peacefully pleasant woman had saved her life, and perhaps others, with simple soap and water. Oh, and her nasal swab results? Positive for anthrax. Multiple spores had taken up residence in her nostrils. Not enough to make a healthy young person sick, but enough to prompt Stephanie to share with us her belief that faith in God saved her. I thought she might be right. But just to make sure, to this day, I still instinctively wash my hands after handling mail.

HAND HYGIENE WASN'T THE ONLY REMNANT OF MY EXPERI-ences in the fall of 2001. My role as night shift commander during the investigation of the 9/11 hijackers' presence in South Florida, immediately followed by running the protracted crime scene searches at the anthrax site, wreaked havoc on my health. The FBI didn't ordinarily function like a police department with established night and day shifts, each with their own command structures. Instead, if something happened after hours, which was often the case, everyone just rolled with it. If it meant getting out of bed at 3:00 A.M. for a kidnapping, you did it. If it meant working all weekend to disrupt a terror plot, you did it. When that special circumstance was resolved, you'd get time off and catch some sleep. That was unless special circumstances became the status quo. For me, the status quo went on way too long.

The HAZMAT search at the AMI building was a daytime operation, so my circadian rhythm tried mightily to readjust. I went from drinking almost no coffee to several cups a day. Once home at the end of very long days, I would try to decompress, then crawl into bed for the night. Again, the phone would go off—with FBIHQ almost always on the other end. This time, the callers were usually analysts working the HQ night shift and prepping for the director's morning briefing. Often, some detail they needed was for the "PDB," the President's Daily Brief. The answers to their questions were mostly included in Miami's daily summary, but apparently they needed to hear it from me. This was no longer about simply not sleeping enough. This was now about not sleeping at all. For weeks. Something was wrong.

I assumed my body clock would return to normal and the sleep I desperately craved would mercifully arrive once we wrapped up the anthrax operation. I was wrong. Night after night, I stared at the ceiling. I got up and read books or watched TV. I tried exercise and over-the-counter sleep aids. I eliminated caffeine. Nothing. I had returned to the office but felt like I was moving through water. Although I didn't understand it at the time, I had developed chronic insomnia. I started researching how long a human can go without sleep. Once I realized that I couldn't solve this myself, I found a doctor who specialized in sleep disorders. An overnight sleep study, with leads and sensors stuck to my skull and elsewhere, confirmed what I already knew—things were messed up. I was grateful that the doc got it figured out and had me quickly back on track. Now I never take sleep for granted and have learned to practice what's called good "sleep hygiene," including adherence to consistent bed and waking times and a regular nighttime routine. Consistency works when you can make it happen. You just have to make it a rule, not an option.

FBI manuals contain seemingly endless guidance for just about everything. The guidance helps maintain consistency. There is even a protocol that says an agent should never let the gas gauge in their bucar slip below a quarter of a tank. That's just good common sense for anyone in law enforcement who might have to unexpectedly engage in a prolonged chase, an emergency response, or impromptu surveillance. But it's also smart on a more figurative, personal level. We all need to maintain some reserve in our body's fuel tank. We can't run on fumes for very long without risking engine damage. Looking back, I should have called time out and asked for help. Too often we delude ourselves into thinking we're the only ones capable of doing something, but we're not. Even more often we think there's shame in admitting we can't go it alone, but there isn't.

Almost a year after our collection efforts at AMI, it was time to go back in and do it again, this time under far less pressure. New techniques for gathering samples and new scientific methods of identifying and assessing the composition of anthrax spores meant that it was worth one more shot to confirm or discount our theories. Besides, despite our unsuccessful attempts to track the discarded package from the now-empty parking lot dumpster to area landfills, we still hadn't given up on finding the deadly envelope. The second collection effort was even longer and more exhaustive than the first. FBI Miami's ERT, now augmented with a full Hazardous Material Response Team from Quantico, spent two sweltering weeks in August making four hundred building entries and taking over five thousand samples. This became the largest hazardous materials crime scene search in American history. But humans weren't the only ones trudging in and out of the AMI building.

One day, outside the relative comfort of our air-conditioned trailer, I caught a split-second glimpse of something waddling down the parking ramp into the AMI garage before it vanished. I thought the heat had gotten to me. I asked someone next to me if they had seen it. "Yep, it's a possum. He's found his way in and out of the building." I was glad the FBIHQ scribe wasn't shadowing me on this one. The Bureau's deadly force policy didn't cover anthrax-coated marsupials fleeing into the community. Satellite news trucks and international camera crews had returned to the site to document our second effort in the building. I had visions of a CNN story about a poison possum terrorizing some nearby playground. No one felt good about it, but we all instinctively knew what had to be done and that it had to be done humanely and quietly. We found a local veterinarian who agreed to trap and euthanize the critter. Rest in peace, possum.

In the grand scheme of things, the possum decision wouldn't even be worth retelling. The decision took us about two minutes. It paled in comparison to the hundreds of far more weighty calls we were making every day. But it's emblematic of a bigger point related to consistency. The reason we could so quickly and instinctively agree on this decision wasn't because it was trivial (except for the possum) but because the art of decision-making becomes second nature in the FBI. The longer you're in the Bureau, and the more responsibility you take on, the more you learn to quickly, consistently, and systematically assess available information, alternative options, and second- and third-order consequences, all while data is flowing at you like water from a fire hose. This is true whether you're a seasoned agent on the street, an experienced analyst in a field office, or a veteran executive at HQ.

Decision-making skills aren't developed in a vacuum. As I experienced in the Bureau, there was a rhythm of regular, often daily briefings at all levels. Something happened when everyone had to consistently and concisely communicate to their boss and their peer group exactly what was happening in their cases, their team, their field office, or an entire national program. Each briefing became a class on decision-making. You weren't just learning what was going on with your team, you were learning how good and bad decisions were made. Suggestions, options, guidance, and cautions were tossed around and people generally didn't hold back. Even at a field office squad level, informal exchanges among agents in the open squad areas could change the entire approach to a case.

At FBIHQ, the regular battle rhythm of morning briefings to the director and evening briefings to executive assistant directors weren't necessarily popular. But there was a beauty and simplicity to establishing a rhythm that went beyond mere routine. I'm not talking only about briefings. It's larger than that. I'm talking about developing a system in your life, your work, or your studies, and sticking with it if it works, or tweaking it if it doesn't. A consistent system. Not just winging it.

Finding protocols and practices that work and jettisoning those that don't also help to preserve what really matters. It also serves to signal when something isn't quite right. During the 2019 impeachment hearings in the U.S. House of Representatives, we saw dedicated career government professionals, one after another, testify that what was happening in the Trump White House was so beyond established principles that it represented a national security threat. Those witnesses weren't malcontent bureaucrats upset that the status quo of foreign policy wasn't being followed. In fact, those professionals were patriots who identified trouble when they realized a kind of shadow government was operating outside of all norms. These loyal men and women weren't part of a "deep state"; to the contrary, they were career professionals who comprised the state.

Don't get me wrong; consistency should never be confused with rigidity. In fact, bureaucracy at its worst is mired in a morass of useless, outdated rules and regulations. The worst kind of bureaucrat is the one so wedded to how they are doing something that they've forgotten why they do it that way. The FBI may have "Bureau" as its middle name, and it may have its fair share of frustrating processes, but it is pretty darn good at realizing when it needs to change and at rewarding those who make those changes. In fact, while the agency revised how it rated its employees several times during my career, the version I liked best was the one in place near the end of my tenure. Among the several criteria used to assess everyone's performance was a category called, "Flexibility/Adaptability." Successful organizations and people remain faithful to their code even as they adapt and transition how they carry it out. This might even mean that you redefine your entire approach in order to remain consistent with your values. That's what the FBI had to do after 9/11. After that national crisis, flexing and adapting meant surviving.

THE FBI WAS REELING FOLLOWING THE DEVASTATING ATtacks of September 2001. It was clear to anyone with a television that U.S. intelligence and law enforcement agencies needed to change how they did business if they were to remain true to their mission of protecting the nation. We needed to transition from an investigative agency that was very good at telling you what happened and who did it, to a predictive intelligence agency that could stop something before it happened.

As is usually the case with strategic change, realizing you need a new approach is quite different from implementing that approach. And while the Bureau was designing its new master strategy, power brokers and policy makers all over Washington called for the FBI to fold. I'm not kidding.

Commissions were created, white papers written, and think tank conferences convened. Most of the questions being asked about U.S. intelligence were reasonable: How could we have missed this? Did the CIA tell the FBI everything it knew? Did the FBI heed the warning signs spotted by its field offices? Were there simply too many intelligence agencies? But some of the questions fired at the Bureau were at best misguided, and at worst, rooted in power grabs and personal politics. I know you're shocked that power and politics would ever motivate Washington politicians.

People in high places were even questioning whether the FBI should continue to exist. Many of those who asked that question wondered whether the Bureau had too much on its plate. The FBI is the nation's primary law enforcement agency responsible for investigating violations of over three hundred different federal statutes. The FBI is also a member of the U.S. intelligence community responsible for leading both counter-terrorism and counterintelligence investigations, and for collecting intelligence in support of every intel agency. Its agents and analysts work drugs, bank robbery, crimes on Indian reservations, and hundreds of other violations, all while hunting foreign spies and international terrorists around the globe. Yet those who questioned the scope of the Bureau's mission didn't understand that the breadth of that mission made the FBI stronger, not weaker. Now we needed to show them.

While still investigating the 9/11 attacks and devising a complete overhaul of the agency and its priorities, the FBI also had to fight for its survival. Some were calling for the FBI to split into two different agencies—one criminal and one intelligence. Others demanded the Bureau be lumped into the hastily formed Department of Homeland Security and its 240,000 employees in twenty-two distinct agencies. The fight was led by Director Robert S. Mueller III, who took the helm just two weeks before 9/11. As a former federal prosecutor, U.S. attorney, and assistant attorney general, Mueller understood the unique strength inherent in the connectivity and synergy within everything the FBI did. Now all he had to do was convince the naysayers.

Some who called for the Bureau to split in two became convinced they were wrong when they heard from our friends in the U.K. and Canada. That's how our two closest allies do it: they have a big police agency with guns and handcuffs, and they have another clandestine agency that handles domestic intelligence and security. The Brits have MI-5 to secretly counter spies and terrorists, but MI-5 needs to call the appropriate police department, like the Metropolitan Police ("the Met") at New Scotland Yard, or a Special Branch unit in some other police department, when somebody needs to be arrested. Our neighbors to the north have the Royal Canadian Mounted Police (RCMP) to work criminal cases against people identified as national security threats, but those cases often start with RCMP's counterparts at the Canadian Security Intelligence Service (CSIS). Have a couple of beers with those folks and ask them how efficient it is to put up a wall between different agencies that often aren't allowed to even speak to each other. They'll tell you.

I saw this problem up close and personal when I headed counterintelligence. The U.S. intelligence community received a highly sensitive tip that a Royal Canadian Navy intelligence officer was working for the Russians. Sub-Lieutenant Jeffrey Paul Delisle was assigned to a secret military intel center in Halifax and had way too much access to classified reporting from all the "Five Eyes" allied nations (America, Canada, the U.K., Australia, New Zealand). In a clear breach of the security protocols agreed on by Five Eye nations, Delisle was somehow able to search for any secret document related to Russia, transfer it to a USB, stick it in his home computer, and transmit it to his Russian handler. The United States and its allies were hemorrhaging our most sensitive Russian reporting for as long as five years. As soon as we learned of Delisle, we knew we had to tell the Canadians and stop this guy. Easy, right? Not so much. Not when dealing with a system that's so very different from ours. The details are still classified of how and when we secretly told CSIS the bad news. But it's no secret that the Canadian intel agency wanted to take a crack at confirming our information before the RCMP got involved. The problem arose when it came time for someone to put Delisle in handcuffs. As the Canadian newspaper the *Star* eventually reported, "Canada's spy agency clandestinely watched Delisle pass top secret information to Russia for months without briefing the RCMP—a previously unknown operation that raises questions about whether the naval officer could have been arrested sooner."

The news report continued: "The spy agency [CSIS], acting on legal advice, opted to keep its investigation sealed for fear of exposing a trove of Canadian and U.S. secrets of the intelligence trade in open court proceedings. In a bizarre twist, it fell to the FBI—not CSIS—to send a letter to the RCMP spelling out how a Canadian was pilfering extremely sensitive information, including highly classified U.S. material." Someone had to call Canada's cops. Strangely, that task went to me.

I wrote a simple letter on FBI stationery to the RCMP explaining that Jeffrey Delisle was a spy. I flew up to Ottawa and sat in a conference room with RCMP officials and verbally briefed the Mounties. Now the RCMP had to start their own investigation to be used in court. Again, the cycle started from scratch, all while Delisle continued to spill everyone's secrets to the Russians. This was taking so long that we considered luring Delisle into the United States so we could arrest him on our own charges. FBI director Bob Mueller even placed a call to his counterparts in Canada and torqued up the pressure for someone to put an end to the madness. The end couldn't come fast enough.

The longtime Russian mole inside the Canadian military

intelligence center was finally arrested by RCMP on January 13, 2012. Delisle became the first person in Canada to be convicted under their Security of Information Act. He pled guilty and was sentenced to twenty years in prison. Although he was granted full parole in 2019, life as Delisle knew it—he received about $110,000 from the Russians over the course of almost five years—was over for him when he was arrested. More important, the Five Eye nations had lost a treasure trove of sources and techniques. Next time you hear someone suggest the FBI should be split, you have my permission to tell them the Delisle story.

As Director Mueller moved to preserve the FBI, he instructed the entire Bureau to prioritize pure intelligence collection. HQ gathered up hundreds of examples of terrorism or espionage intelligence reported by the FBI's criminal informants, as well as examples of criminal intelligence reported by national security sources. Colombian drug sources provided details on Muslim terror groups training in South America. Russian organized crime informants coughed up eastern European terror cells. And on and on. Briefings on the beauty of the Bureau's unique mission were provided to key congressional members on all the oversight committees. And a plan was drafted to completely remake the FBI.

Since the Bureau and its sister agencies were accused of not connecting the dots to prevent 9/11, the FBI would hire a slew of new dot connectors. More important, these intelligence analysts (IAs) would drive the direction of case openings, informant development, and program strategies. Tactical IAs would sit elbow to elbow with agents in squad bays to guide specific casework. Strategic IAs would draw connections across the work of the entire field office and beyond to the intelligence community. Thousands of entry-level hires would be recruited from the nation's top campuses with the prime qualification being a proven ability to ingest huge amounts of data and make sense of it. An entire new division at FBIHQ, the Directorate of Intelligence, would be formed to ensure the success of the program. After a protracted battle, the White House and Congress bought into the plan and signed off on the necessary funding.

Counterterrorism would become the FBI's number one priority, not just at HQ, but in every single field office. No longer could a smaller field office claim that their territory had no ties to terrorism and that, say, white-collar crime was their top priority. Every office would get a dedicated counterterrorism squad and go through specialized subject-matter training. A massive shift of resources would realign agents and IAs from criminal squads to terrorism squads. In Miami, an office traditionally focused on narcotics, several drug squads were realigned to create a multisquad JTTF. The plan to remake the Bureau also meant that special agents, traditionally the gun-and-badge-carrying stars of the show, would learn to view IAs as partners, not as their support staff. Today, new agents and freshly minted IAs train together at Quantico for the first time in the Bureau's history. Before they ever hit a field office door, agents and IAs have already learned how to work alongside one another, one team, one fight.

Retooling a machine as massive as the FBI was a bit like turning an ocean liner in the middle of a monsoon; you knew it could happen, but you didn't know how long it might take or how many would survive. Some grizzled old-timers who spent long and colorful careers chasing fugitives and bank robbers decided the change was a little too much for them and threw in their retirement papers. Some veteran IAs, facing much tougher performance and training requirements, chose to leave or accept other roles. Most agents and analysts grasped the gravity of the moment in history and committed to the new Bureau. Like that ocean liner in the storm, the course wasn't fixed or steady and had to be frequently corrected. But one by one, field office after field office made the transition. Our team in Cleveland was one of the first to make it happen, and I was proud of them.

FBIHQ deliberately decided to transition the field first. After all, the field was where the proverbial rubber met the road, and it was the field, not headquarters, that would have to prevent the next terror attack. However, that meant that for a protracted period, in some cases over a year, some divisions at FBIHQ were still not "walking the talk" within their own hallways. This wasn't because anyone in Washington was refusing to make the necessary changes, but rather, because of a host of transition scheduling, financial, and operational reasons, there were some divisions that hadn't yet pulled the trigger. In fact, the Counterintelligence Division (CD) had still not made the change when I got "the call" from FBIHQ. It was time for me to leave Cleveland, head back to the Hoover building, and return to my first love, counterintelligence.

BEFORE I EVEN ARRIVED IN WASHINGTON, MY NEW BOSS, the executive assistant director of the National Security Branch, loudly and clearly communicated my mission during a quick phone call: completely transition the Counterintelligence Division to the new Bureau. "If you think you can do it," he said, "the job is yours. If not, tell me now." I told him I was up for the challenge. After about three months serving as deputy assistant director, I was promoted to AD, the role sometimes referred to as the nation's top spy catcher. The official word came from Director Mueller as he walked past me in an inner corridor along his seventh-floor suite of offices. Without breaking stride, Mueller looked at me and said, "I'm giving you the AD job." It was a three-second drive-by promotion.

I had big shoes to fill. The retiring AD was a friend of mine, a brilliant CI expert and Harvard grad I had twice worked alongside in earlier assignments. There was certainly nothing broken in the CI Division, but the program needed serious updating. Unlike the field office I had just left, I found the IAs segregated from the agents, occupying separate spaces and even separate floors. I asked the IAs to show me their top analytical reports in each program. Their reports were interesting academic studies but had little or no connection to catching spies. I asked the agents if they had read any of these top analytical products or even knew they existed—nope. It was time to move some furniture and knock down some drywall.

There's always resistance to change in any outfit. Doing it right means investing time in hearing everyone's concerns and letting them play a role in how the change happens. Change shouldn't be something that happens "to" people, it should be something that happens "with" people. It's crucial that everyone involved understand that adapting doesn't mean an abandonment of values or mission. To the contrary, the proposed changes must reflect how those changes are not only consistent with your values but vital to preserving them. There was some pushback to colocating agents and IAs, even more than I saw in the field. Some agents didn't fully understand what value the analysts would add, and some analysts feared they would lose their independence. I decided to create a new deputy assistant director role; the first nonagent, senior IA to hold that position in the division. This was more than mere window dressing; it was a genuine statement that we were committed to the new way of doing things. When the dust settled, the plan started slowly falling into place, and intel analysis started quietly driving our strategy and our vision.

There was another kind of stovepipe segregation that got my attention. The spy war was increasingly being played on a cyber battlefield, but at FBIHQ, the spy catchers and the computer geeks resided in two entirely different divisions. Over the years, our adversaries, including China, Russia, Iran, and North Korea, admitted to themselves that they could not beat us in a traditional boots-on-the-ground battle. They saw the ease with which American forces breezed into Iraq, rained hellfire on Afghanistan, and picked off one terrorist leader after another with tactical drone strikes. This freaked them out. In response, our enemies came up with another strategy to hurt us, or as the Chinese say, to "win without fighting." Their strategy was asymmetric and cyber-driven. But because of overcrowding, the FBI's Cyber and Counterintelligence Divisions weren't even in the same building.

After the terror attacks of September 11, 2001, the Bureau understandably declared counterterrorism its top priority across the FBI. There was a seismic shift in resources aimed at preventing the next act of terror on U.S. soil. Very few inside the Bureau dared suggest a rethinking of this prioritization, even with years of distance from that devastating day and with the impressive successes in dismantling the hierarchies of al-Qaeda and ISIS. But as I took the helm of the Counterintelligence Division over a decade later and saw the growing complexity of the foreign intelligence threat, I voiced my concern.

Every year the Bureau reevaluates its ranking of investigative priorities. When it was my turn to weigh in on the discussion, I made a case for flipping CT and CI at the top of the list. I showed the increasing economic impact of foreign operatives ripping off trade secrets from U.S. companies across all field offices, the growing aggressiveness of intelligence officers operating in the United States, and the complex and hybrid nature of the threat, with expanding cyber operations, front companies, and nontraditional actors. I feared that our response to 9/11 had served to almost permanently distract us from the "other" national security threat—the one that kept growing while the CT threat was waning. While we were neutralizing terrorists, the Russians, Chinese, and others were rolling out their new intelligence strategies virtually unchecked. But I wasn't telling the folks on the seventh floor of the Hoover building anything they didn't already know.

Because of the nature of and secrecy around CI work, very few members of Congress, let alone the public, fully grasped the foreign intelligence threat, at least back then. Even merely implying that foreign spying was a greater threat to our democracy than terror groups could sound like we were somehow disrespecting the thousands who died on 9/11. Yet as politically unpalatable as it sounds, a terrorist organization was unlikely to dismantle our democracy. And while the unspeakable horror of 9/11 briefly united us as a nation, the secret work of adversarial governments would soon have us deeply divided. The Bureau's priorities would remain unchanged on paper, but there was agreement that this expanded intelligence threat demanded, and would receive, greater resources and efforts.

The FBI still had a kind of artificial wall between the Cyber Division, which addressed online spying, and the Counterintelligence Division, which worked traditional cloak-and-dagger espionage. But foreign intelligence services couldn't have cared less about our bureaucratic organizational structure. In fact, they may have benefited from it. State-sponsored hacking, use of social media platforms, and outright denial of service attacks were becoming the new game in town. Once again it was time to move bodies, furniture, and walls. In close partnership with the head of the Cyber Division, we formed a hybrid unit staffed by both traditional CI specialists and Cyber Division computer experts. Making this change, like the much larger transition of the FBI, was clearly consistent with preserving the FBI's mission for years to come. And the FBI's successful transition to defend its mission meant that it could successfully adapt to defend America. One team, one fight. And the battle continues.

Although it may seem counterintuitive, consistency and change are joined at the hip. To preserve our core values, we all inevitably must change, adapt, and transition to new ways of preserving and promoting what we hold dear. The FBI redefined itself from an investigative agency to an intelligence-driven domestic security agency. That change was entirely consistent with what the FBI has always been—a defender of the Constitution. The Bureau didn't transform just so it could survive, it adapted so it could continue to protect our nation against new and different threats. Successful people, businesses, and teams don't view change as a threat. Rather, they understand that adaptation is the means by which they can maximize their mission and remain vital, relevant, and consistent with who they are.

OPS PLAN

U NDER ENOUGH STRESS, PEOPLE, TEAMS, BUSINESSES, and even nations can lose the ability, and even the will, to spot and defeat threats to what they hold dear. Maintaining that capacity requires consistent vigilance. It also requires a plan. In the FBI, an operations plan (or "ops plan") is drafted before any significant arrest, tactical assault, major event or exercise. It might take the form of a quick verbal brief among agents huddled outside a fugitive's hideout or require an elaborate written product in preparation for securing a global event. The bottom line is that if a mission is worth doing, it deserves a plan. And any endeavor worth planning should reflect the values of the people and organization involved and be performed in a way that increases the likelihood of success. That's what the Seven C's of Code, Conservancy, Clarity, Consequences, Compassion, Credibility, and Consistency are all about. This book is an ops plan for getting that done. Now let's outline your execution of the plan.

Establish your core values. Once those are in place, your code should almost write itself. Does your team value honesty? Make it against the rules to lie, especially about substantive matters. Should everyone be treated with equal respect? Have a written policy that addresses discrimination and harassment. Is there a goal to eliminate cheating on sales reports or expense vouchers? Spell it out. Crafting your code is relatively easy—it's keeping the code that gets complicated. That's where the other C's come in.

Conservancy means that maintaining code is a team sport. Doing the right thing should not be someone else's responsibility. Whether it's your corporate brand, your campus environment, or your family reputation, hold everyone accountable for preserving what counts. That might mean you need to set up or enhance a reporting mechanism so people are empowered to let leadership know what's happening. It also may require that you rethink who conducts internal inquiries, audits, and disciplinary matters so that everyone takes a turn defending against conduct that undermines the greater good.

Clarity mandates that your code is communicated clearly and frequently and is easily accessed. Don't play games with vagueness or "wiggle room." If your employees perceive their code of conduct to be a mystery, you can rest assured that they'll default to doing their own thing. Treat lapses in desired behavior as teachable moments that can be carefully communicated as conduct to be avoided. Reward and celebrate exemplary performance that most reflects your values. Signal the kind of conduct you're aiming for by modeling it yourself.

Consequences may be unpleasant, but they're essential if your code is going to last. Yet consequences so harsh or random that they're perceived as unjust can quickly undermine an organization. Ensure transparency and openness by publishing your version of due process and sticking to it no matter what. Similarly, when it comes to consequences, the best surprise truly is no surprise. Let everyone know the range of discipline they could face for specific misconduct and apply those standards fairly and evenly.

Compassion must be a component of every discipline decision. People abandon collective values if they discover that compassion isn't one of those values. The easiest way to make compassion instinctive is to build it right into your deliberative process. Require decision makers to always consider both aggravating and mitigating circumstances before acting against a team member. Always give an individual the opportunity to present their side of the story, including any pertinent personal factors.

Credibility is the lifeblood of the FBI; without it, the mission fails. Doors might get slammed in agents' faces, sources won't get developed, judges might not sign warrants, and juries could reject expert testimony. Restoring damaged credibility can take years, even decades, if it happens at all. This is as true for individual leaders as it is for the organization they lead.

That's why any entity striving to succeed must treat threats to its reputation as threats to its existence. To do that, first ensure that your internal process for preserving values is one that people can trust. Next, remember that no one, inside or outside your team, will fully believe in your values if they don't believe in you. Last, when you screw up, admit it, get it out in the open, map out a path to fix what happened, and provide updates on your progress.

Consistency means acting in the same way over time to achieve the desired effect. What's the desired effect? Optimizing performance by embedding your values in everything you do—not just when it's convenient, but especially when it's hard. And even when you think no one's looking. That's when consistency really counts. Yet, even when there are proven best practices, we still go in some other direction when stress, temptation, or both get the best of us. To counter that human tendency, establish values-based protocols and policies for everyone to follow. It might seem like drudgery, but it makes decisions, particularly during crises, so much easier. But simply having rules of the road won't keep us from veering off the highway. You'll need guardrails. The FBI's highest-profile mistakes happen primarily when its leaders act contrary to their own rules. So make it harder to fail by implementing persistent practices, like daily or weekly briefings, peer review, redundant oversight, crisis management teams, and other built-in systems that help make doing the right thing instinctive muscle memory.

The FBI has an admirable system that helps it stay squarely focused on values even under pressure. The Bureau is at its best when identifying and countering threats, not just threats to its own internal code, but to our nation's values. That doesn't mean we shouldn't hold the agency accountable, demand improvements, or question its methods or its failures when the FBI gets it wrong. But repeated attacks on an institution that defends our democracy threaten more than just one agency; they jeopardize the very values that the institution embodies.

Our democracy is still a young, vulnerable experiment in preserving the values that define it. It's not unlike whatever organization you belong to or are trying to lead. No matter how long your team has been around, its survival and success can't be taken for granted. It requires a code and a way to keep that code. When it comes to preserving our grand experiment of democracy, we should all share the same values, the same code. Now *The FBI Way* of preserving its values and ours has been shared with you. It can become your way, too.

ACKNOWLEDGMENTS

I WOULD BE TRAMPLING ON MOST OF THE SEVEN C'S IF I LED any reader to conclude that the concepts composing *The FBI Way* were mine. In fact, I would have failed as an author. I've simply organized these concepts and conveyed the lessons I learned, often the hard way, from an outstanding organization and some exceptional people, during my twenty-five-year journey in the Bureau. As those who worked with me in the earliest years of my career will attest, I did not enter the FBI with inherent leadership expertise. I got it wrong plenty of times. The principles of values-based performance excellence that I learned along the way came from the people with whom I was privileged to have encountered.

My first years in the FBI's Atlanta Division were blessed with squad supervisors who served as mentors and models of excellence. In my first assignment to the Counterintelligence Division at FBIHQ, close colleagues were a constant source of strength, and humor, while we charted the course of our program in a seemingly post–Cold War world. In San Francisco, my teams began teaching me it was more important to lead people than to manage programs. Back at FBIHQ in the Office of Professional Responsibility, I learned that knowing what not to do was as vital as learning what should be done.

At FBI Miami, the experienced staff that I oversaw, and the senior executives who supervised me, taught me the value of getting out of my comfort zone and relying on others. The people and offices I audited as the Bureau's chief inspector taught me far more about our organization than I could teach them. When I led the FBI in northern Ohio, the talented men and women of the Cleveland Division, and our partners at the U.S. Attorney's Office, showed me what talent, tenacity, and midwestern work ethic were all about. Last, the honor of serving as assistant director of Counterintelligence allowed me to learn the value of an entire intelligence community partnered together to defend America against all threats, foreign and domestic.

There were also people beyond the Bureau who made this book possible. In fact, some of them made my career possible. My partner in life, the "special spouse" to this special agent, embodies each of the Seven C's more than I ever could. Her imprint is on this book. Our two sons, now with families of their own, sacrificed time with their father and geographic stability, yet became men of quality who strive for excellence every day. Their own kids, my young grandchildren, supplied much needed "joy breaks" during long days of manuscript drafting.

I met literary agent Peter McGuigan of the Foundry long before I decided to write this book, and I was impressed by his energy and enthusiasm. When it came time for me to defend and extol the work of the FBI, Peter was the right choice. Next, my friend, writer Ellis Henican, graciously added some punch to my book pitch. At Custom House/HarperCollins, vice president and editorial director Peter Hubbard was invaluable in helping me organize the right words, in the right place, at the right time. He reminded me a bit of the dedicated English and writing teachers who influenced me in high school and college. Copyeditor Laurie McGee polished the final product with precision. I did the bulk of my writing in the relative solitude of three places: mostly at the Pima County Public Library, Dusenberry-River, in Tucson, Arizona, where I was often the first one in to grab the corner table; then at a quiet place across from the beach in Carlsbad, California; and finally at the Lucky Dog Inn in St. Petersburg, Florida. I recommend them all.

As required of former FBI employees, this book has undergone a prepublication review to identify any potential disclosures of classified or sensitive information but was not reviewed by the Bureau for editorial content or accuracy. The FBI does not endorse or validate any information that I described in this book. The opinions expressed are mine and not those of the FBI or any other federal government agency or department. The factual descriptions of FBI investigations I did not directly work on are based primarily on public news reports, interviews, and other source reporting, and not on information I learned while serving as an FBI special agent.

As you can see from the previous paragraph, I'm still adhering to *The FBI Way*. That's because it works for me. Better yet, it works for America.

INDEX